Living at Hollis

Audrey Breshears

Audrey Breshears 5-19-14

To Perk Dickson

May we meet at the pearly gates.

Introduction

Sparks flew as Danny tossed another tobacco can onto the fire. Rain dripped from the brim of his hat and off the steep roof of the old cabin and ran down the mountain in rivulets, carrying with it the ashes of the past.

We bought the old Whitcomb place in 1999 in the midst of the Y2K era. Many people thought with the stroke of midnight December 31, when the new century began, computer glitches would grind the world to a stop and there would be ensuing chaos. There was a lot of talk of 'bugging out' to a safe place away from civilization, and the location certainly did fit the bill.

The farm was a fixer upper. An old cabin in a state of disrepair with no electricity, no running water, overgrown fields, and a washed out driveway presented us with several years worth of work, and we started by purging the contents of the house and burning the rubbish in the yard.

The turn of the century was uneventful, but our time spent at Hollis was not.

Table of Contents

The Store

Hollis is easy to miss if you are driving too fast. It seems to be little more than a store, a church, and a green highway sign declaring its presence, but looks are deceiving. Located in the Ouachita Mountains in central Arkansas, Hollis, like many other southern communities, is rich in history, culture, and personality.

"Hey, Connie." The screen door slammed behind me as I went into the Hollis Country Store.

The proprietor answered, "Hey, how ya doin'? Y'all on the way up to the cabin?"

"Yeah, gotta go feed the goats," I said.

Connie Hawks, with her short cropped gray hair and talk to anybody charm, rang up my Coke and cheese crackers. I had something I wanted to ask her.

"I'm thinking about writing a book," I said, as if I knew how to do that. Connie nodded her head.

"About Hollis. Darrel Humphreys was at the house the other day, and he told me that a writer named Charlie May Simon lived out here a long time ago."

"Yeah, she did. I've got one of her books," she said.

"Really? Well, when I found out that she lived out here, that got me to thinking about Hollis, you know, the history of the community. You think anybody out here remembers Charlie May Simon?"

"Well," she said pushing her glasses up, "Perk Dickson might. He's gettin' pretty old, though. He ain't in good health."

"What's his name?" It sounded like she said Perk, but I wasn't sure.

"Perk Dickson. His name is James, but ever'body calls him Perk."

"Oh." I wrote down his name.

"He's on oxygen," she said. "He's up in his nineties. If you want to talk to him, you better hurry up and do it."

"Okay," I said. I planned to call him very soon.

"You think anybody else would want to talk to me?"

She thought for a moment. "Yeah, you could talk to Harold Shepherd, and maybe one of the Crains." Connie gave me several more names and looked up their phone numbers in a comic book sized phone book and read them to me.

"1727," Connie said. "is Perk's number."

I was confused. A four digit phone number? Then I

realized all the numbers in Hollis had the same prefix, so the locals didn't say the first three numbers, just the last four.

"Oh, okay," I replied.

Connie licked her fingers and turned the page. She gave me a couple of more numbers.

"I bet the store has a lot of history, doesn't it?"

"Oh, yeah," she said, pointing to a copy of a newspaper article on the wall. "It's on the National Register of Historic Places. So's the bridge."

Hollis Country Store sits near a bridge spanning the South Fourche LaFave River. Connie rummaged around behind the counter. She handed me a copy of a newspaper article featuring her store.

"The original portion of the Hollis Country Store was begun in 1931 and finished the following year. The building was built using local stone laid in a random pattern, a type of construction found in many parts of Arkansas. The building was built by Mike Gross and William (Bill) Furr. Mike Gross operated the store along with the Hollis post office, which was on the south side of the building. In addition to operating the store, Gross was a country doctor who was often called upon to pull teeth in the surrounding areas. The small shed behind the store, which housed a Delco (generator) for generating electricity, was constructed about the same time as the store.

"In 1940 Mike Gross sold the store to Dennis and Lillie Crain, and they renamed it the Crains Store. While they owned it, Lillie was in charge of running the post office. The Crains also lived on site in the rear portion of the building. In the late 1940's and early 1950's, Dennis and Lillie's daughter, Gulelma, and her husband, Loyd Hawks, took over operation of the store. Gulelma was paid $8 per month for working in the store. In addition, Dennis and Lillie Crain's sons, Gerald and Harley, helped with the store's operation, although they never took ownership of the building.

"In order to provide more services to motorists traveling on Highway 7, Dennis Crain had two tourist cabins built south of the store in the early 1950's. Bert and Bart Graves built the cabins, and bathrooms were added between the cabins in the late 1960's by Dennis Crain and John Whitcomb.

"In the early 1950's, the store building was expanded

with a large addition that was constructed on the north side of the building. Also in the 1950's, space in the store was further expanded through the construction of frame additions on the south and rear sides of the store building.

"It is likely that the picnic shelter was constructed at the same time that the stone addition on the store was constructed. The same style siding was used in the gable ends of both structures, and Dennis Crain was involved in its construction. George Hooper also helped build the shelter. The picnic shelter and the well were used both by the patrons of the store and the occupants of the tourist cabins. Prior to the construction of the current shelter, an ice house stood on the site.

"After Dennis Crain's death, Lillie sold the store to their son Harold and his wife Louise. They built the brick house just to the north of the store in 1980. In 1989, the store was again sold, this time to Loyd and Gulelma Hawks' son, Berl, and his wife, Connie. Although Berl died in 1999, Connie and daughter Kim, continue to run the store, which is open seven days a week, providing goods and services to the people of the Hollis area."[1]

Mr. and Mrs. Humphreys

Several days after I met with Connie, I visited with Gene and Ann Humphreys. Like many of the residents of Hollis, they lived on Highway 314, west of Highway 7.

When I pulled in the driveway, Gene was standing on the steps waiting for me. He was dressed in blue jeans and a long sleeved khaki shirt with two front pockets. He wore wire-framed glasses and had his gray hair in a sideways part. He waved and smiled.

I got out and we shook hands as we introduced ourselves. He opened the door to his home for me, and as I entered, I saw his wife, Ann, standing in the living room. She welcomed me and asked me to sit down. I took a spot on the sofa, and we began to talk. I needed to spread out my three ring binder and have a place to take notes, so I asked if we could move to the dining room table.

Ann offered me a drink, and she brought Gene and me a cold can of Dr. Thunder and a glass. We poured as I asked how they had met. Gene laughed and looked at his wife who had taken a chair across the table from me. She was a trim woman, neatly dressed in a modest skirt and a crisp blouse. Her hair was perfectly coiffed. She smiled a tight lipped grin and looked down at her drink. Gene wore bilateral hearing aids but still struggled to hear. Ann shouted my question to him. He turned his empty can of Dr. Thunder in his hands, smiled, and said, "At the picture show."

Gene had recently broken up with a girl. One evening he went to Aplin, a community near Hollis. He spotted Ann and her sister outside the theater and struck up a conversation. As they told me of their first encounter, I tried to imagine what they might have looked like in the late 1940's. I pictured a tanned young man with dark hair and a shy young woman in a print dress, smiling at each other.

Ann said she and Gene dated for a while, and then they were married at the Perry County Courthouse in 1950.

Gene, born in 1927, is a lifetime resident of Hollis. His family homesteaded the land where Gene and Ann currently live. The original portion of their house was moved from the area flooded by Lake Nimrod in 1942. (Lake Nimrod was built to control the Fourche LaFave River.) They bought the house for nine hundred dollars and moved it to its current location. They have improved and added onto it over the years. It rests in a peaceful setting on their farm near the south fork of the Fourche Lafave River.

Like many men from Hollis, Gene made his living in the woods. He worked for the Dierks Lumber Company then for the Weyerhauser Lumber Company in the logging industry. Gene and Ann also owned a commercial chicken house.

Hollis is home to several chicken houses. Most of them now are dilapidated and falling in on themselves, like cakes that have fallen in the oven.

Ann Humphreys managed their chicken house for some thirty years. She said her son Darrel hated the chicken house chores. "He spent most of his time runnin' from one door to another, tryin' to get him some air," she said. *Maybe that's why he became a helicopter pilot*, I thought. *Lots of fresh air.*

I asked Gene if he liked living in Hollis, and he said, "Man, I sure do." He said they had left the area once to live in Oregon for about a year, but soon returned to the peaceful valleys and quiet mountains of Arkansas.

When Ann was a girl, her family raised cotton, and

other crops. Gene remarked, "This is not no farmin' land for cotton. One time everything burnt up, and we went to Dumas (in southern Arkansas) to pick cotton and we stayed in a old shotgun house. I was about twelve years old, and once I picked a hundred and thirty two pounds of cotton in one day." He smiled proudly.

Since I knew nothing first hand of picking cotton, I raised my eyebrows and nodded and tried to look duly impressed. "Wow," I said. I figured the cotton probably weighed more than he did, which *was* impressive.

While Gene and his older brothers all went to pick cotton, one brother stayed home to watch the place. Their hard work paid off. "On payday we turned it all over to Dad to pay the bills and we come out pretty good."

Cash crops like cotton were needed to make money to buy the things that families couldn't grow on their farms. Many folks grew crops to sell in addition to what the family would need to sustain itself, but that was hard work, and barely profitable. That's where moonshine came in.

I asked Gene, "Did you ever know of anyone running 'shine?"

He laughed and said, "Used to, a lot of them did.

They'd build 'em a whiskey still, they called it, out in the woods, as far back in the dark places as they could get it. They'd make their brew and everything and they'd cook it off. There was one fella that lived down the road here, close to where that store is. He had him a rig back up the holler there; my older brothers found it," he smiled and said, "They drank it!"

"We found another one, me and my brothers, over there one day. This man had a little rig way back south of the river up there. We went up there, and we got us some beer. I think I must have got a little bit happy or something because something got a hold of me." He giggled mischievously and Ann, who seemed to find little humor in this commented, "I imagine." I wiped the grin off my face.

"There's another place over there that was on top of Oak Mountain," he continued, "back west there, that man, he kept it all the time. He died, but he had his wife and one boy that was in college and another little boy. We was over there working just above the house and we didn't know anything was wrong. We been marking timber some way and there was three or four of us together, and we got to throwing rocks down in the woods and one of the boys walked off down yonder and he come back and he said,

'They's whiskey down there.' When we found out about that, we left. And just a few days (later), the revenue men came in down there, and they had it piled all around there in five gallon jugs. The revenue men got that boy. I think he was going to make a doctor. He was paying his way through school with that. I don't think he ever done much time."

Gene's experiences with moonshine occurred when he was a teenager, but he recalled a time when he was a just a boy. "The river's right over here, and there's a big hole of water. There's an old road that goes right by the river. A bunch of people came in there camping, and they might of stayed there a week to camp and fish and swim, and I guess picnic. I went over there one time after this bunch had been there, and I got to looking around. I don't know how come me to be out there by myself," he said reflectively. "And there was some light bread, (a term for sliced bread bought at a store) laying out there somebody had throwed out. Well, that was a good thing to us then. I looked all around, and I didn't see nobody." He paused, letting me anticipate what he would say.

"I ate the bread! It was good!" Ha! I knew it. "We wasn't used to nothing out of town. We just had biscuits all the time." He laughed, staring at the napkin holder on the table, but he was not seeing the napkin holder. He was seeing himself eating that light bread on that creek bank and remembering how good the bread, eaten in secret, had tasted.

Our conversation turned to me.

Danny and I own seventy acres straddling a mountain called Stover Shack Ridge, known to the community as the Whitcomb place. I asked Gene what he knew about our property. The first thing he wanted to know about was our water supply.

"Do y'all use the water out of the well, have a lot of water?"

"Oh, yeah. We never have any problem."

"I witched that well," he said. "I was scared to death there wouldn't be much water, that high up."

"How do you witch a well?" I asked. I had heard of it, but never seen it done.

He grinned and said, "Would you want to try to witch one?"

"Sure!" I said. I knew that well witching is the practice of trying to locate underground water before a well is dug, but I didn't know the technique.

12

We pulled on our jackets and went into the yard. It was obvious that it hadn't been too long since Gene had witched a well because the tools were readily at hand. He picked up two L-shaped welding rods about three feet long, with handles about six inches long.

He said he used to use a forked wooden stick, but had switched to using the two metal rods because he thought they worked better. He handed them to me and showed me how to walk slowly with the rods pointing parallel in front of me. He steered me in the direction of the well house, and completely on their own, the rods crossed when I walked over the vein of water near the well.

"Am I doing it?" I asked.

He laughed. "There it is!"

He talked while I walked around with the witching rods.

"No telling how many wells I've witched in this country," Gene said. "I've missed a few. Sometimes you can't tell if they's one or two veins (of water.) One might be lower in the ground than the other. I've been fooled a few times."

Well witching is an inexact science. I'm glad it worked on our mountain, and I was glad to have met the man who found our water.

Connie, John, and Aubrey Gene

I had arranged to talk with Connie Hawks about her life in Hollis. On the afternoon of our appointment, I swung open the wooden screen door to find two men sitting in the chairs near the register talking with Connie. A row of four chairs face the cash register where the hanger outers sit while they drink their coffee or Cokes. Instead of gathering around a literal cracker barrel for conversation, like they did in the old country stores, they just rotate through and sit in the chairs for a while to catch up on the gossip.

I slid open the door to the drink box and got my Coke (even though it was a cherry Dr. Pepper) and took it to Connie to pay for it. Every soft drink is referred to as "Coke" in Arkansas, i.e. What kind of Coke do you want?

"We've been talking about you," she said and introduced me to Mr. John Young and Mr. Aubrey Ballew. Word was getting around that I was writing a book. I was pleased (and a little embarrassed) that they had been talking about it. I was, however, glad that they were in the mood to talk about Hollis.

I sat down in one of the chairs with the men while Connie manned the register and took care of the lottery ticket buyers and Coke/candy bar customers. I was amazed at how many folks bought a lottery ticket in the hour or so I was there.

They told me about the history of Hollis, including where Highway 7 used to lie and where the store was prior to its present location. As they talked, they began to recollect stories they had heard as children.

Johnny Young asked me if I'd ever heard about the two brothers who met an untimely end in a hand dug well.

"Did you ever hear the story about when Babe and his brother Sam Humphreys died in the well up here on the mountain, on Cove Mountain?"

I shook my head no.

"When I was just a little boy and we lived down there in Long Hollow, Daddy worked with Babe and Sam for Dierks Lumber Company, and I remember we had the old crank telephone, and the line just went up the holler there, mostly family was on the line, and it went to the tower. If you wanted to talk to the outside world, you called John Lancaster at the tower, and he got a message out. I don't know how he got it out, whether he had a radio or a phone line, but anyway, we had to call the tower.

"Daddy hadn't been home from work all that long, and John called us and I guess everybody in the area.

"Well, what had happened, Babe, Inez Humphreys' first husband, was going to clean out the dug well. They used to have to do that on a lot of wells, clean the muck out, you know."

"Dug" wells, as they are referred to, are bigger in diameter than the modern machine-drilled well. Contaminants such as methane can accumulate, and a near zero percent oxygen level can exist in the depths of a well.

"Sam told him to wait 'til he went to get a lantern. He was going to let a lantern down in there, and their thinking was that if there was poison gas down in there, the light would go out, but in reality, if there's no oxygen, it will go out, too. But there's not necessarily gas, but maybe a poisonous atmosphere.

"Anyway, Babe didn't wait. He lowered himself in that well while Sam went to get the lantern. He got down there and because of lack of oxygen, he was in trouble by the time Sam got back. Anyhow, John had called people, and everybody was converging on the mountain. Babe's brother Sam lived right up here, up Highway 314. I guess

17

he was one of the first there, and he went down to get his brother. Rather than tie himself to the rope somehow, I think he had a loop, and he put his foot in it, and he was just going to hold onto the rope and let them pull him up. Well, he got up part way and he passed out and fell back into the well. And then Perk Dickson (one of the first on the scene) went down and got them out. As I understand it, it was injurious to Perk, to his health for quite sometime.

"As having worked on the bottom of these dams in the discharge tubes I've worked on, I remember that we had to test for dangerous organisms that grow in that environment that are detrimental and can kill you, and I suspect that could have been something like that, who knows?

"And get this: Perk Dickson ends up marrying Babe's widow and raised his kids."

This is a locally famous story. I was anxious to hear it firsthand.

Mr. Young also related a humorous incident that happened while he was working on a crew that cleared the trees to put in power lines.

"You know that made me think back. Let me tell

you what happened."

It was hot summertime when he was on the clearing crew. They worked their way along, up and down mountains, cutting trees and brush as they went, to make way for the poles to be set to hold the electric lines.

"We had to carry all that equipment, picks, shovels, crow bars, buckets of that stuff we treated the poles with.....we got down to South Fourche and there wasn't anyplace to cross. So we stripped off and swam that stuff across the river. "Just so happened that one of the bosses of that company showed up to check on us and he had a camera. We didn't realize it. He took pictures of all that!" He laughed and adjusted his cap. "Course, we tried to take it away from him and couldn't. He took them back and showed everybody, I'm sure, in the country. But, of course, we had a big time swimming that stuff across. That's why we did it."

Aubrey Gene Ballew, the other man visiting with me is retired from the United States Forest Service and is quite knowledgeable, not only about the lay of the land, rivers, and mountains but of the community as well. He told me about landmarks, locations of community cemeteries and where folks lived. He is a lifelong resident of the community.

"What makes somebody an outsider?" I asked.

"Somebody that you don't know their folks," he said, and laughed loudly to cover what may have been offensive, seeing that it applied to me, but I took no offense.

I nodded my head and thought to myself, "Well, I'm an outsider, then," even though we had owned property in the community for thirteen years. I realized I can never be considered, or have the right to be considered, a true member of the lifers, the dug in, the blue bloods of Hollis.

The Shepherds

As I drove up the driveway to Harold Gene and Opal Shepherd's house, Opal came out on the stoop to greet me with grandson Sage on her hip. She led me into her living room that was scattered with Sage's toys and sippie cups. It reminded me of the way my house looks when my grandkids have been there. Opal set Sage down and he smiled at me shyly from behind his grandma's legs.

As we were getting acquainted, Harold appeared from the back of the house carrying a large rolled up paper. He introduced himself and shook my hand then sat on the couch. Opal did most of the talking with a few interjections from Harold here and there. The topic turned to homesteading.

The large roll of paper was a painstakingly created map of the Hollis area. Mr. Shepherd had documented the dates and names of the original owners of farms homesteaded in the area, complete with color coding. He pointed to the map as he studied it through his bifocals and explained his and his wife's ties to Hollis.

As we examined the map, I searched for an answer that had arisen during my research.

Charlie May Simon, the author who had lived in Hollis in the early 1930s, had mentioned in one of her books that her grandfather had homesteaded in the valley. I wanted to find the name of this ancestor, and here it was on Mr. Shepherd's map: Benjamin Hogue.

Charlie May Simon wrote some thirty books, the first of which she penned while living on Rocky Crossing. It was titled Robin on the Mountain. I had become very interested in her works and her life. I bought several of her books and then went online to learn about her life.

According to the Encyclopedia of Arkansas History and Culture, "Charlie May Simon (1897–1977) is among the state's most prolific major authors. Known primarily for her children's literature, with just under thirty books and with numerous short stories to her credit, Simon had a long career writing for adults as well. Additionally, she is known as the wife of Pulitzer Prize–winning poet, John Gould Fletcher. Her work in the field of children's literature has been honored in Arkansas since 1971 by the annual presentation of the Charlie May Simon Book Award.

"Simon was born Charlie May Hogue on August 17,

1897, not far from Monticello,(Drew County), to Charles Wayman Hogue and Mary Gill Hogue. She was named after both her parents, according to Southern tradition. Her father, a tenant farmer at the turn of the century, was also a teacher and an author. His book, *Back Yonder, An Ozark Chronicle*, published in 1932, recounted his youth and was a successful book in its day.

"The Hogue family moved to Memphis, Tennessee, when Charlie May was three years old. Educated in the Memphis Public School system, she also attended Memphis State University (known then as Memphis Normal School). As a young woman, Hogue attempted to publish a novel but was disappointed when a publisher rejected the manuscript. She turned her attention to art studies. Hogue's first marriage was to Walter Lowenstein, a wealthy heir of a Memphis mercantile business, but she was widowed while still in her twenties. She wanted to enhance and expand her perspectives in the world of art, so she used the financial settlement from her first marriage and moved to Chicago, Illinois, and later to Paris, France. In Paris, she met and married Howard Simon, an artist who would become the illustrator of her books. The two married in 1926, and she became Charlie May Simon, the professional name she used for the rest of her life.

"Simon returned to Arkansas with her husband. This was during the time of the Great Depression, and money was scarce. The two resided in a mountainside log cabin that they built themselves in Perry County with help from neighbors. Simon planned the cabin, drawing the outline for the walls with a stick in the dirt. In the 1930s, she returned to writing, in part because they needed the money and because she wanted to tell of the Ozark way of life and the strong people who lived it. The Depression still had the nation in its grip, and Simon's strong work ethic served her well. Simon enjoyed the hard work of the homestead, but her husband did not. She and Howard divorced, and though he returned to Paris, he still served as illustrator for her books. Simon's first major work for children was *Robin on the Mountain.* It was published in 1934 and is considered by many to be a classic in the field of children's literature."2

As we discussed the fact that Charlie May Simon had lived in the area, Opal Shepherd recalled hearing her mother in law, A.B. 'Ussie' Hawks, talk about attending a dance given by the Simons. She and her brother Loyd Hawks went to the all night square dance.

"Ussie could remember all about the dress that Charlie May Simon had worn. I don't remember its color, but it was fancy, long, dressy – bought way out from here – it really caught her eye. I think some of the furnishings in the cabin caught her eye, too."

Ms. Simon had lived in Memphis, Chicago, and Paris, so it's probable that she was indeed wearing a dress "bought way out from here."

"I don't really know how old she was. Old enough to go to the dance and remember it," Opal continued. "I reckon they rode a horse down there. She remembered this dress and how different this woman looked. She said that they stayed all night."

Even though Charlie May Simon was born in Arkansas, her life had shaped her in ways that made her quite different from the residents of Hollis.

Opal said, "Ussie was young and as the night wore on, she got tired of watching the girls dance and flirt. Her brother was a little bit older than her and the young women were really interested in him. I reckon she went on to bed and went to sleep. They had everything pulled back, I think she got under a table to go to sleep. But she was quite in awe, and Charlie May Simon was very friendly, and good to her."

The dance at Charlie May Simon's cabin understandably made a lasting impression on Ussie. She told the story often enough that her family remembered it long after her death.

Charlie May's book about the time period in which she lived in Hollis was called *Straw in the Sun*, published in 1935. In it she describes the square dance that she had given for the community. There was plenty of moonshine, dancing, fiddling, and food. All the furniture was moved to the sides of the room and into the yard to make room for the party, and everyone arrived in fresh clothes with their hair fixed and their shoes carefully cleaned and polished.

Simon also speaks of choosing the land she would homestead. Her grandfather, 'Old Doc Hogue,' had meandered through the area, eventually choosing an area in the valley below Rocky Crossing, where Charlie May's place was, to stake his claim. When Charlie May and her husband, Howard, returned to Arkansas in 1931, they claimed sixty acres in the mountains. She describes building the cabin and living there with two children from the area who came to live with her. Vannie was a young teenager who traded labor for education, and Bob was an orphan who had run away from a children's home in Little Rock and just showed up at her place. He provided all the wood chopping and gardening chores that a twelve year old could manage. She never mentions having a husband in the book.

Howard Simon also wrote of the homesteading experience in a book called *Cabin on a Ridge*, in which he details how the community gathered for a 'house raising.' He also chronicled the way of life of the mountain people in quite a different way than his wife did. Like Charlie May, he wrote the book as if he lived in the cabin on Rocky Crossing unmarried.

Charlie May Simon and Howard Simon were not country people in the sense that most people who lived at Hollis were. They had lived in New York City, Paris, and Chicago. Their experiences were much more diverse, and it surely impacted their lives in Arkansas. Howard mentions that the reason he decided to homestead in Arkansas was that hard times had fallen on the country and he was selling no art. He was looking for a way of life that required little or no capital to survive. When times got better, he left Hollis, as did Charlie May.

As I chatted with Harold and Opal Shepherd, their

daughter Mandy sat nearby on a computer, making copies of pictures and looking up facts on the internet. I asked her what it was like to be a young woman living in a remote place like Hollis. She said that it was hard being a teenager in Hollis, because there's just not much to do. But in retrospect, she said that she was glad to have grown up in Hollis rather than in city like Little Rock.

There may be a stark contrast between Little Rock and Hollis, but the little town has had its share of colorful characters. One of these is Opal Shepherd's great grandfather, Andrew Miller. The following newspaper article appeared in the September 24th, 1881 edition of the Little Rock paper:

"SHOT LIKE A DOG. Perry County Comes to the Front with a Characteristic Case. Perry County contains some excellent, law-abiding citizens; but the fact cannot be gainsaid that she also numbers among her population some murderous desperadoes, whose continued existence is living evidence of the inefficiency of the law, or their lack of execution. Scarcely a week passes but what the public press is called upon to chronicle some damnable deed of crime that sends a thrill of horror through the land and awakens a spirit of distrust and fear against the entire state. As before remarked, there are some good people in Perry County, and they owe it to themselves, to their country and the state to see that the murderous element is put down – exterminated. They can hope for no peace, prosperity, or progress until this is done; and the sooner, the better.

"From a gentleman who arrived in the city last evening, the following facts in reference to the latest killing in that county were learned: a few days since, a difficulty occurred between Andy Miller and Joe Miller, two farmers residing on South Fourche creek. The trouble originated about some hogs belonging to Joe Miller breaking into Andy Miller's field. Several times, while Joe was absent from home, the hogs broke into the field and Andy chased them out. Joe, on returning, expressed a desire to see Andy not interfere with his hogs, and so informed Andy. Hot words followed on both sides, but they perpetrated without coming to blows. A short time afterward they met in the road. Andy Miller was armed with a double barrel shotgun. A few words passed, when he raised the gun and fired, lodging the contents, a dozen or more buckshot, into the breast and face of his antagonist. Death was instantaneous, and the murderer quietly walked away, leaving the bloody remains of his unfortunate victim lying on the road."

Opal recalled the details of the incident passed down through her family.

"Andrew Miller served in the Civil War on the Union side, on the Calvary. In 1880, he and his brother Joe Miller got into a fuss and Andrew shot and killed Joe. They had to have a trial in Perry County over the situation and the fact he was a Union soldier, and everyone in Perry County was Confederate, it took over three days to seat a jury. I would of thought they would have just jerked him up and done something with him, but no, he had lawyers in Little Rock that tried to keep him from being hung, is what my daddy said. He lost a whole bunch of his land trying to pay the lawyers.

"The dispute was over hogs. His brother was Joe Miller and his hogs got into Andrew's corn field, and I think they'd had some problems before about it. From the family stories, I think Andrew killed Joe's hogs that were in his cornfield.

"Andrew was down on the riverbank doing some clearing, and when Joe found out about his hogs being dead, he came down there to confront him, and he had a chopping ax raised up coming at Andrew. Since Andrew had just come out of the war, he happened to have his gun right there with him, and he just raised his gun and shot his brother.

"It was kind of self defense on Andrew's part, but he was the only one there to tell the story. He had to go to prison; he was sentenced twenty one years, and he served fourteen.

"He broke out of the Perry County Jail one time; they were holding him there until he could go to trial. He broke out, he and two other men. Daddy said that Grandma Miller went down to visit Andrew, somebody took her in a wagon, I guess, but Andrew had told her some kind of acid to buy that would cut the metal bars into. She rolled the glass bottle with the acid in it in the top of her stocking to hide it; of course her dress was way down long. He also told her to bring a turkey wing for a fan."

"Mandy, go back there and get that turkey wing fan," she said. Mandy got up and left the living room.

"You've got one?" I asked.

"Oh, yeah."

Mandy came back. She handed me the fan and Opal explained how the joint in the wing was singed to hold it open. It was huge.

"Well, Grandma Miller went to the jail and took the acid and fan to him. There is no official record telling exactly how they got out. He stayed out a good long while, about a year. He hid out on top of Hooper Bluff (an outcropping of rocks overlooking South Fourche LaFave River.) They had little cotton houses where they stored the cotton until they could get enough to take to market, and he hung out down in the cotton houses on his own land. His wife would bring him food and stuff. When they finally caught him, he was on top of Hooper Bluff. You can look down from it and there's a great big field down there that he owned, and he could see the sheriff with the dogs tracking him, and that's where they caught him.

"He went to the penitentiary and he tried to escape and he was shot in the leg. He said they didn't do one thing to help him whatsoever. It was really cold and in the winter time, and all they did was just picked him up and threw him into the cell to let him live or die. He said a black man slept close to him that night and kept him warm enough to keep him alive. If it hadn't been for that, he would have died.

"He wrote his wife and told her that he would not

ever try to escape again, that he just couldn't make it; the gunshot had damaged him, so he told her to marry again because she owned all this land and she had several children and she needed someone to help her farm the land. He knew this man well, that she married, so he might have suggested him, I don't know. She married a John England, and they had two children together, two daughters." After fourteen years, the governor of Arkansas pardoned him. When he learned he was pardoned, he wrote home."

She went on.

"Andrew Miller wrote a letter to John England, who was married to his wife, and told him he was coming home and he had better get gone. So, John England took his two daughters and went to Oklahoma. He left.

"She had legally married John England. Then when Andrew came back, he and she didn't really get remarried legally until he started to try to draw his pension from the military, the Union Service that he was in. This was in the early 1900's. They lived together as married people, they didn't have any more children. Those two girls came back from Oklahoma to live with their mother and he raised those two girls."

Some years later, they found Andrew dead in the barnlot, not sure if one of the fine horses he was known to have kept kicked him, or if he died of natural causes. His wife died later the same year.

Opal laughed, pushed up her glasses and said, "That's not all of the story!"

She said Andrew wanted to draw a pension for war injured veterans even though he had not been hurt in the Civil War. He devised a scheme to claim that the gunshot to his leg sustained during his escape attempt had happened during a skirmish at Dardanelle. The claim was investigated by a special examiner with the Department of the Interior, Bureau of Pensions. A copy of the letter sent back to Washington DC relaying the findings of the investigation reads as follows:

"This pensioner, Andrew P. Miller, lives at Hollis, Perry County, Ark. It requires a whole day and part of a night to reach his home back in the mountain range on Fourche La Fave. I was obliged to walk up four mountains then ride about twenty five miles in a buggy. When I called he was away from home. And I took this deposition of his present wife. He lives in what is generally regarded as the roughest place, I understand, in Arkansas. His home cannot be reached and return there from any Railroad station in one day. It would require over a day if worked alone."

This letter, although somewhat of an exaggeration, describes the remoteness of Hollis pretty well. The place exudes a quiet, almost surreal atmosphere, where it is easy to imagine that the world is not on fire, that neighbors still take care of each other, and that the greatest problem to be addressed is finding something to shoot for supper or getting to the store to buy coffee and flour and get the latest news of the community.

It doesn't take much to really connect with the stories of Andrew Miller hiding out at Hooper Bluff or to imagine the hollow echo of chopping axes as the settlers cut virgin timber to make a field or to hear the scuff of shoes on a wooden floor dancing to fiddle music at an all night square dance or to see the sun rising through the mist on the South Fourche River.

When I sit on the riverbank, the only sounds I hear are whispers as the tree tops murmur to the water. They seem to speak to each other in hushed tones of another time, giggling with their memories and their secrets, and I only catch snippets in the conversation. The ripples smooth out and disappear into the depths and the trees raise their heads and arms back to the sky, pretending they can't talk, that they never saw me. I am listening, though. I am listening.

Perk Dickson

When I called Mr. Dickson to ask for an interview, I could tell I was in for an interesting experience. He spoke loudly with a country air, with a teasing lilt. He agreed to speak to me; I was pleased and anxious to meet this local hero.

I climbed the steps to his house and knocked on the door. "Come on in!" He shouted from inside. I opened the door and stepped into the living room. Mr. Dickson was a thin balding man, sitting in a wheelchair with oxygen prongs in his nose and tubing that wound around his ears and met at his throat in a clear, skinny necktie. There were no foot rests on the chair; they would only get in the way as he pulled himself around with his feet. An unmade hospital bed occupied one end of the living room.

"Come pull this chair right over here," he told me, motioning to a spot next to his empty bed. He positioned me where he could talk to me but still keep sentinel on the driveway through the large plate glass window.

I obeyed.

I told him about the book and how I wanted to write a history of Hollis through the words of its residents. I told him where our place was and how we acquired it.

He, in turn, told me a little about his background. He was born in Hollis in 1921, making him ninety one years old at the time of our interview.

I asked how he came to have the nickname Perk. I was thinking it had something to do with his perky personality.

He laughed and said in a loud, almost shouting voice, "I want you to know, I can't think of those men's names over at Plainview. Came up here and camped over by the low water bridge over by the Hawks School. Came over and camped and fished. One of 'em's name was Perk and one of 'em was Arlie, I believe. Well, me and my brother younger than I was, you know how kids will be, I called Rob Arlie, and he called me Perk. That's the way it got started right there. Rob didn't keep his, but I kept mine, and I still got it."

I told him I had heard that he had retrieved some men out of a well. He rubbed the white stubble on his chin as he recalled the incident, his voice softer.

"Well, I was boarding with them (Babe and his wife

Inez.) He was a good friend of mine, and still is a good friend of mine (even though Babe Humphreys had been dead many years.) His daddy-in-law, he had them come in there and clean the well out. Well, he (Babe) went down there to clean it out. They went to drawin' him out (from the well) and the poison got him. I don't know how fer, but I know he fell back. Well, his brother came in, Sam, he was the first one there, and he went to get him out. He got down in there." Now Sam and Babe were both in the well, taking in the foul air.

"I got there and went to gettin' her man (Inez's first husband, Babe) out. Then Sam, I was a drawin' on him, it was just me by myself and he weighed more than I did; he was too fer down, I didn't have power enough. I'd just reach down and raise up and step off and hold it and reach and get me some more (rope.)

"And he said, 'Hurry up and get me out of here!' and I says, 'Sam, ain't you tied?'

'Naw.'

"I said, 'Boy, you ought to be tied.' About that time, he fell back. Got him in that fresh air and he fell back. Well, by that time there was getting to be several people come."

Perk asked for help from one of the first men to

arrive. He knew someone would have to actually go down in the well to get Sam out since he had lost consciousness. In his desperation, Perk said to him, "Go down in there and put this around Sam and let's get him out of there."

"Noooo, I'm not going." The man wasn't willing to risk it.

"Well," Perk continued, "Nobody to get him out and I knowed it. Somebody had to get him out. I said to myself 'The good Lord with me, my hope, I'm gonna get that boy.'

"I told them fellers over there, 'Tie me on there; tie me where I won't come a loose and I said, 'I'll go and get him.'

"Well, they tied me on. They had a leather belt. I put that leather belt under my arms and cinched it up."

He jumped ahead to the part when he felt himself getting lightheaded from the conditions in the well and cried out for help, omitting the details of what happened in the pit.

"I hollered at them to bring me out. I was so sick, I'd hold my breath a little too tight. I was so sick til I couldn't lay down. I got so sick, I don't know, I can still taste that stuff in my mouth at times." He held his lips in a tight line and looked at his hands in his lap.

Perk had been dangled like a carrot on a string tempting death and yanked from its jaws at the last second when he entered the well and tied a rope around the Humphreys brothers, who were already dead. They were drawn out of the well, and Perk was pulled to safety, but he was sick from the air in the well. I commented that it must have been difficult and upsetting for him.

"Well, the good Lord must have been with me, bound to have been with me." He told me about the aftereffects of being in the tainted well. "I made it pretty good for an hour or two and it got to burning on me. They took me to the hospital down there in Hot Springs. I don't know what they done to me; they put me in the hospital. I woke up the next morning, I don't know what time, but the people here from South Fourche had done come down there. I had my breakfast and they brung me on back home."

The Humphreys brothers were laid to rest, but they made one last visit on the way to the cemetery. "They took Babe and Sam on to the graveyard, but they stopped to show them to their grandma. She wanted to see them; she was bedfast. They took them out and carried them up there for their grandma to see them and then took them on up

41

there and buried them."

Perk went on to marry Inez, widow of Babe
Humphreys, and raise the couple's children. I asked him if
he had it to do over would he go in the well?

He said, "Yeah, they was good friends of mine, both
of them, always had been; we was raised together." Perk
and the Humphreys boys had ties since childhood, and the
brothers had married local girls.

"Sam had married my cousin; Babe had married
Inez. Sam used to come up there when he first went to
courting around with the women pretty heavy. Come up
there and wanted me to shave him. I'd shave him every
weekend. He married my cousin, Ruby," long pause, "And
that stopped all the shaving."

I burst out laughing and so did he.

I remembered someone had told me that Perk might
remember Charlie May Simon. I told him where our place
was in relation to Rocky Crossing. He did remember the
Simons.

He said, "When I was a kid growin' up..." He paused
to think. "Now I've got to kindly recollect, that's the way it
goes when you get age." He collected his thoughts.

"Goin' a fishin, we'd go to Rocky Crossing, go right

down by Charlie May Simon's, down there was an old field down there, and we went and camped, camped down there and fished. As we'd go and come, we'd get drinking water and they's a big spring down there, where we went and camped, too. We'd stop at Simons' and get water, goin' and a comin', drinking water, you know.

"Now that was before this road (Highway 7) was even graveled. It wasn't even gravel, it was just a plain old road. No gravels or no nothing, just a regular old road. It wound around and wound around and came out right down here, hit (Highway) 314. They was ruts, in that old road, that wide (spread his hands about a foot) and that deep, going up and down it. In a car, you didn't have to have no steering wheel, just stay in the ruts." I laughed, imagining the old cars bumping along with its occupants talking and no one driving.

"We lived right up here, right on the road, in a little old pink house. My grampaws and grammaws, both of them, lived right up yonder. Jim Dickson on my daddy's side, and Jim Tillery on my mother's side.

"My daddy had an old T model. He'd go up and get my Grampaw Tillery and my Grampaw Dickson and come down to this little old pink house, and we'd kill hogs." Hog killing was an all day process. "And he'd take 'em back of a evenin'. He'd give them meat and all, you know, dividing."

He remembered a hog killing when his mother had been left home alone to tend to other things. Country people, women included, typically own guns and know how to use them.

"That's when Daddy had gone to take them back; it was dark, and why, someone came in on my mama up there. Well, Mama had the gun, and she got after them, and they got out the back end of the house."

What were they after, I wondered. Money? Food? Didn't matter.

"Didn't know who it was," Perk said. "My dad come in about ten or fifteen minutes later, she told him about it. He got out and went all around the house and couldn't see nobody, so he came on back in. We never did have no idee who in the world it was." Daddy didn't find them because they were long gone. Mama took care of it.

Perk went on, abruptly starting a new story.

"Goin' to church – we'd go to the Valley Home Church up there. That's when my Grampaw Tillery ran the post office up there on 314.

"That's when Mike Gross ran this one down here

(on Hwy 7), that's when they had mules and wagons. My Grampaw Tillery ran that one up yonder (Hwy 314) at Avie, or some funny name, anyway, he run it. They had church right there. Used to have church across the creek over there at Hawks School by the cemetery. Then they moved it up there where it's at now."

Mr Dickson attended school at the original Hawks School. "I had to walk from back this side of Grampaw Tillery's all the way around, walk across the footbridge, the swinging bridge, walk across through there in the winter time. In the summer time, why, the creeks wasn't up. You had a foot log down there, and you could walk down there, it was about a mile, maybe, walk over there to school, but I didn't get to go to school very much."

"How long did you go to school?" I asked.

"Fourth grade. We had to come in and pick cotton and pick peas and everything."

Harvest time in Hollis, like in most other small farm towns, was a time when every family member was called upon to help, even the children. School had to wait. The building was nearly empty or maybe even closed during the time when fields were being planted or crops being gathered. It was just understood.

The restored Hawks School is now on Shepherd's Ford road off Highway 314. It served the community from 1911 to 1949 and the building is now on the national Register of Historic Places. The original Hawks School was built circa 1880 near the Hawk Cemetery. Restoration of the relocated building was completed in 1984. It is a one room school house, white with blue trim, a bell tower, two front doors, and two outhouses.

Danny and I visited the school one afternoon. We pushed open one of the two heavy wooden doors and stepped into the silent classroom. Dust covered wobbly benches faced an American flag at the front of the room where the schoolmarm would have stood. Low angled rays of sunlight filtered through the surrounding trees into long windows with wavy, bubbly glass panes. Specters of past students peered through class pictures on the walls. As I sat on a bench, I imagined myself one of them, doing my best to sit still, listening to the hum of katydids outside in the trees, my rumbling stomach making me think about what Mama had packed in my lunch pail, and hoping the teacher would pick me to fetch some water so I could have a reprieve from the tedium. I thought about how I feigned the need to go to the bathroom when I was in school just to escape for a few minutes, and wondered if the children who sat in this school room ever did the same.

****

As Mr. Dickson and I continued our visit, he reflected from time to time while I waited. He scratched his face thoughtfully, and I noticed that his left index finger was partially missing. I wanted to ask about that, but I never did.

A new story came to mind, and his volume cranked up as he told it.

"We went down there, great big boys, to go a swimmin'. Gerald Crain ran in there and asked his mother could he go, and she said not to get in that big deep water.

"Well, we all went down there, and that's the first place Gerald made for was that deep water."

He shook his head.

"We hadn't much more than got in the water, I hadn't, til Gerald went to hollerin' get him, get him. I was about a year older than Gerald, or two, I made fer him, got him, got a hold of him."

Because the boy was panicking, he struggled with

Perk.

"When he was about to drown me, I'd kick him a loose."

They continued this struggle until Perk was getting exhausted. He tried to think.

"I knowed they was a wedge of rocks in there about that wide (2 feet) in that hole of water somewheres." He would have to release his grip to try to gain a footing. "I'd kick him a loose and see if I could find that rock. I'd think, 'I'll have to just let him drown, I can't help it.' Then I'd think, 'I better get him.' He struggled between exhaustion and his conscience.

"And I got him.

"When I went down, this left foot hit that ledge of rocks. The next time I got him, I come down on that ledge of rocks." He managed to hang on to the flailing boy. "He was just like holding an eel. Boy, I tell you, I had to set down on him, hold him..he was trying to climb out the top of me.

"I told them boys, 'Bring that boat out here!'" He shouted, his face animated, as he relived the moment.

"They said, 'It's full of water! It's full of water! It's full of water!'

"Anything would have holp me, you know, to got him a hold of. I helt him there til I got him straight."

He was breathing hard.

"I said, 'Now, Gerald, we got to walk right down this a way here; you let me lead the way.'

"I could feel the rocks with my feet. I got him out of there and just as quick as I got him out, he headed to the house, and we did, too, the rest of us did. Got up there and he fell with one of them spells on the front porch. We were all up there and I told what happened. One man got up there and mashed a little water out of him, not much, not enough to amount to anything."

Gerald's father was upset with Perk because he laid responsibility for the incident with him.

"Boy, Dennis Crain ate me out. Let me tell you, I just walked off and left him, him eating me out."

Later that night, there was a singing at the Ark School. Perk was a little alarmed to see Gerald and his father there.

Perk said, "Well, Dennis says to me, 'I want to talk to you a little bit.'

"I thought he was going to whup me, what I had in mind. My uncle was standing right there with me, and he

49

come outside with us. We walked out there a little bit, and Dennis said, "Perk, I'm sorry, terribly. I won't never forget the way that you've treated my boy."

"I helped him," Perk said.

His voice changed as he took on the role of Gerald's father.

"I know, I know, you helped him. He's done told me all about it. I've done the wrong thing and I want to apologize to you."

"Well, I says, " Perk spoke meekly. "I just thought I was doing my duty to help him."

"You did," said Mr. Crain.

It was more than duty, though. It was above and beyond; Perk had averted a terrible tragedy.

Poignantly, he concluded: "Gerald was my number one friend."

Perk became pensive. The memory of saving Gerald had stirred others.

"I tell you, I been in some terrible, terrible bad places, shapes, in my lifetime, cuttin' trees offa people...I don't know what's wrong with me.

"I cut trees," he told me. "When I was cutting logs for Weyerhauser, cut two different trees off of two different men."

"Did it kill them?" I asked.

"No, didn't kill neither one of them." He told me of the first incident.

"One of them, I had to have Loyd Hawks, he was the straw boss, he had to hold him, keep him from moving, where I could cut all that stuff off of him, 'fore all the bunch got there, got if off and called an ambulance to come and get him. Well, he got up, got straight in six or eight months."

He went on to tell me about the second time he had to cut a log off a fellow logger.

"Pete Noles, he was a cuttin' down there, and Earl was a scaler, they put him bein' a scaler instead of cuttin' logs."

"Now what's a scaler?" I asked.

"Went around and scaled your logs, see how many feet you cut that day. He come around and was scaling me, and me and him was talking and we heerd somebody hollering 'Help, help.'" He made his voice sound distant.

"Earl said, 'That's Pete!' I grabbed my saw on my back, and I said, 'Go on, Earl, I've got this saw and I'll be right on.' Course, I was there nearly by the time Earl was there. There was that log laying on that man. I said, 'Earl, you go and get the truck and bring it right around there. 'Bout like from here to the edge of my garden there, they was a highline, that you could drive down it. I said 'Drive it down out there and maybe I'll have him up where we can get him.' Okay, he took off.

"I cut twelve foot off of that guy. I think it was twelve, might not have been twelve, might have been more, might have been less, I don't know. Cut that off and I said, 'Now, Pete,' I said, 'You see that log there don'tcha? He said 'Yeah,' I said, 'I'm gonna pick up that log and you slide out from under.'

" 'You cain't pick that log up.' He quoted the trapped man.

"I said," he laughed a little. "I was kindly upset and scared too, you know, I said, 'You slide out from under there when I pick that log up.' I retch down and got that log and picked it up and he skid out from under there. I laid it back down and got down there and got him up and 'bout that time here drove Earl up. Got him in there and sent him on to the hospital."

I said, "You had that super human strength that happens when you're scared."

"I guess," Perk said, and shrugged his shoulders. "I went by there the next day and couldn't even pick the log up.

"I went on a cuttin' logs; I don't know what's wrong with me, I get caught in everything. That very day, my friend, J.T. Wood, let the saw get next to him. I was cuttin' next to him, might have been further than from here to the back of your truck out there, he hollered at me, he said, 'Come here, I'm bleeding to death.' I looked over there, and there was blood squirting from here to that winder." He pointed to the large window in his living room. "I seen I had to do something. I had on boots. Only thing I could think of was my boot string. I took my boot string, pulled it out there, cut it off, and ran over there and wrapped that around that boy's leg. Well, I hollered for help. Got him down there and got him away. They said if it had a been ten minutes longer, he'd done been bled down."

He switched gears.

"Before that, Tom Crawford, my neighbor, good friend of mine, perfect, lived up at Steve. He come down to go cuttin' logs wi' me. We was over there cuttin' logs; I was over there cuttin' one strip, Tom was on another'n, I forget who else, but anyhow there was six of us, six strips on forty acres of land. I's a cuttin', gettin' with it - course you had to stay in there to make a livin' at that time. I was getting with it, he was getting' with it, we was all gettin' with it.

"I heerd Tom a hollerin' and that saw a runnin' some way or another. I looked over there, and he hollered 'Help!'

"Course, I threw my saw down just quick as I could and got over there to him. He let that saw get loose on him, cut him, I mean it *cut* him." He talked through clenched teeth and motioned to the area around his face and neck.

"He was bleedin', oh man, what you talkin' about. I knowed I had to do something and do it quick. I run and grabbed him, I said, 'Tom, I've got to get you to the truck.'

"I grabbed him; we had to get over a log or two to get down there. Got down there and my boss said, 'You take him on down there to the camp and let them take him on.'

"I just drove off and him a talkin'. That's the way you treat your men; don't care nothing for your men." He spoke out loud what he had thought of his boss.

"I took him down there; he'd done bled down on me. That's when they had the train hauling logs from

Jessieville to Mountain Pine. Dog if the train had me blocked there for about five minutes, other side of Jessieville there, and I was in Tom's truck. Boy, I opened her up, but I knowed to not drive too fast, I had to be safe a doing it.

"Got him down there to the St. Joe. I went in there and told them, 'I'm gonna have to have some help out here.'

"They said, 'Aww, it's surely not that bad.'

"That nurse, when she saw him, said, 'Bring a wheelchair, just as quick as you can! And call the doctor!' He shouted, imitating the nurse's urgency.

"In that seat, he was just as limber as a rag. I thought, 'I got to ease this door and get a hold of him; he'll fall out.' He done bled down. I retch in there and got a hold of his britches.

"I said, 'Now open the door and help me get him.'

"They did, and we got him out and got a hold of him and set him down where we could drag him over there in that cheer, drug him over and took him in there. By that time the doctor had gotten there.

"He said, 'Are you the man brought him down here?'

"I said, 'Yeah.'

"He said, 'Don't you leave 'til I talk to ya; I'll be back down here in a minute.'

"He was bloody as a hog; he was in the operation room hisself.

"I waited around there, and they got him all cleaned up, warshed up, got that stuff a runnin' in him.

"That doctor come back and said, 'Go on back out there and get his wife and tell her. You go out there and find his teeth and bring them down here. I've got to have it. He's got his jaw cut into or broke, and I've got to have it.'

"Okie Doke. Here I went.

"Come by and got (my wife) Inez, I said, 'You come and get me now, and leave this truck up here for her (Tom's wife) to come to the hospital.' She did. She got Henry and herself and went to the hospital. I let Inez out and I went back over there looking for his teeth (dentures). I found them and took them down there. The doctor had to have them to straighten his jaw back up."

At this point, Perk chuckled. He said, "I was always full of my bull, and he was too, for we liked that bull. I got down there, and he was way yonder better'n he was. I went to bulling him a little. I seen I had him, and I said, 'You've always pushed me around, got my toes cut off and everything else.' I said, 'Now what about you?' "

"He went to laughing and said, 'Don't! It makes me hurt.'

"I done made good then; I seen I had him." He smiled broadly, thinking of the living, breathing, bandaged man in the hospital bed.

He explained the toe comment.

"I got my toes cut off, cuttin' logs out there, two of 'em cut off out there. I lost a week or two of work out of that."

I knew working in the log woods was hard work, and dangerous, but it made a living for many Arkansas families. It still does. It is not for sissies.

Perk began to recollect happy times.

"I've had lots of good times in my life. I'd go to the dances every Saturday night, over here at Plainview at the VFW. Man, I've made many a step over there. When I was growing up, a kid about eight, ten year old, my grandmaw and grandpaw had one of them old timey cut records about that big around, put it on there and turn it, you had to crank it to make it go. They got me started a dancin'. My Aunt Alice, she liked to Charleston, and that's something I never could do. I tried at it, but I never could do it like it ourght to be done. But any of the rest of it, I could do one or two steps of it. This was all before I got married. Oh, I enjoyed dancing! I loved dancing.

"I went over there since I got married, went over here at Nimrod. Friend of mine, Elzie Owens, you probably didn't know him or heerd of him, we went fox hunting. One night they was giving a man a supper there who had been gone away. We stopped in there and that man came out there and he says 'Come in here and dance a little and get ya a piece of cake and a piece of meat!' So much for fox hunting.

"Okay. We went in there. There was a little woman just about your size," he threw a gesture my way. "Might not have been as big, come around, and she says to me, 'Perk, I've heard you was a pretty good dancer. Let's dance this one.' They told 'em to play the music, and we did. Boy, I tell you, we burnt that floor up there for a little while. They wanted me to dance two or three times. I told them, 'I'm fox hunting over here and my wife's at home, I'm supposed to be a fox huntin' and here I am a dancin!'"

He laughed and then became more serious.

"This has been a beautiful, beautiful world to me. I

been from the east coast to the west coast, but I love Hollis, Arkansas." He has made his home in Hollis for nearly all his life.

Perk told me about his wife, Inez.

"My Daddy thought lots of her. He said she'd do more for him than I would, and I said, 'Well, I'm proud you think that.'"

It seemed Perk thought his dad may have thought more of Inez than of his own son, but he didn't say that out loud.

He took care of his father as he died.

"I set up with him eighteen months in there, and worked ever day. Ever third night for eighteen months, with my daddy right in there. Well, just before he died, I called Dr. Pennington, and Dr. Pennington said, 'He's all right now, but I'll have to take the weight off ya." I supposed he meant putting his father in a hospital or nursing home. I said, 'Dr. Pennington, do you reckon he took the weight offa me when I was growin' up?'

"No," he spoke for the doctor.

"I'm not takin' the weight offa him. If he dies, as I know he is, he can die right in there. That's where he died. I was workin' the day he died, 10th day of July. They called me from my job and I got here about an hour before he died, I guess. He didn't know it, but I got here before he died.

"But he was just a passin' through, just like me and you are. Just a passin' through. That's what old Jay Harkey told my Grandpap Dickson, and all of 'em, said, 'We're not here to stay, we're just a passin' through, that's all.'

I nodded and almost said Amen.

He went on. "God is the one who's got the bull by the horns. He's the one that's got it. You can look up if you want to and see if the Bible ain't a fulfillin'. Look at this fightin' and look at this killin' and everything else over there. He speaks of this, he speaks of all of this.

"I tell ya, I was baptized years ago. I was going with this old widow woman. They thought she talked me into the notion to join the church. She did not, I'll tell you that, she did not. I joined the church and everybody thought I was going to marry her, just to tell you the truth about it, I came within a spat of doing it, being honest about it. But anyhow, we didn't.

"Well, the next week or two, the old boy that was baptized with me was drinking whiskey down here. I thought, 'Uh oh, I'm in the wrong family, the wrong side of the boat.' I didn't say nothing, I just had it up here. I said to myself 'I've either got to get away or else.' I just didn't know what to do. Fooled around til he got me back on that dadgum stuff, sucking the bottle, beer bottle. Got back on that. That's the worst thing I could have ever done. Got back on the bottle. If I'd have stayed on the Lord's side, I probably could have walked through the Pearly Gates, you cain't never tell. I'd like to walk through them. I'd like to. I'm praying to God that I can. I'll tell you something else that has gone agin me - hearing, talking, seeing. I cain't see and if you caint see, you cain't read the Bible. If you cain't hear, you cain't hear the Bible without them hollerin' at you. But I'm gonna die anyhow. I'm just a passin' through."

Seems to me that Christians who recognize the inevitability of death and what awaits us on the other side are more comfortable with passing on. I think Mr. Perk is one of those.

I asked him if there was one thing he wanted me to put in my book, what would it be? He thought for a moment and said simply, "I love the Lord."

And with that, another story popped into Perk's head.

"My Grandmaw Tillery, she got down sick with

pneumony, and we lived down this side of the Valley Home Church there, there where Bert Tillery lived, up on the hill. Mama was already up there, staying up there and helping her. Well, me and my daddy and all the kids was up there. My daddy sat up 'til I don't know what time of a night, and a comin' back, course there was those ruts in that road that deep, I'll tell ya! And that wide. And the Warners, they lived in that little old house down there, and they had a little old black three-legged dog. Well, me and Dad, comin' down here, he was on one side of the truck ruts, and I was on the other side. I don't know why 'til yet I wanted to get over there with him."

He laughed softly.

"When I went to get over there, that's where that dog was layin'. In them ruts. He come out of there, I hollered, and I tell you, I believe if I had a heart, it'd a come out!"

He looked at me for my reaction.

"Scared me so bad! That guy went to hollerin' and a pattin' his britches. Well, that made it worse!"

I laughed. I could just see the barefoot boy running around his father's legs, being chased by a yapping three legged dog.

Changing the subject, I asked if anyone he knew had made whiskey. Perk became sober. (Sorry, I couldn't resist.)

"Oh, they had to back in the Depression for a person to have any money. Over at Ola, my Uncle John, he'd take it over there and sell it to a man that ran the store, and he'd sell it there at the store. One time my daddy made it. He sold seventy dollars worth. That's a lot. And that was the first pair of Sunday slippers that I bought. He bought them right then.

"In them days, they brought your clothes and britches up about that high, knee britches, not down long like they are now.

"My mama and us bunch of kids lived up here. She wanted our picture took. She made us walk down there to Aint Ollie's. Mama didn't think nobody could take pictures but Aint Ollie. I don't know how I got my britches tore, but I got 'em tore right there (near his front pocket).

"It ain't been eight or ten years ago I seen that picture with that hole in my britches, and I still remembered that." I asked if he got in trouble for getting his pants torn.

"Naw," he laughed softly."But that makes me think

of I time I did get in trouble. I don't know what it was about, fighting I guess, I was pretty bad to fight. Mama was gonna make me come to her, give me a whipping. I knowed I was into it, but I wouldn't come to her.

" 'You better come to me!' " She retch down and got a rock. " 'I says you better come to me.'

"I wouldn't do it. Circle round, circle round, I finally thought I seen a way to get out of there without getting hurt. I whirled and run, and she did throw it though; she hit me on the ankle with that rock, knocked me down. Didn't hurt as bad as I let on like it did. Boy, I let on like it was broke. Course it scared her, you know. When Mama said come to her, you better do it. When she got a hold of you, she didn't care to whip you, neither. But Mommy wasn't stout enough to whip me much.

"In '38, Christmas Day, my mama died. I was seventeen. I had to help with them kids. I was the oldest one at home. My oldest brother was in the CC camp."

A clock chimed in the background as he studied his tobacco spit cup.

Civilian Conservation Corp

"I got in the CC camp. My daddy got me in the camp, and I worked at Mt. Idee (Ida) at the CC camp. Well, I got out from down there and got in down here at Hollis and spent the rest of my time down here at Hollis."

I asked how he liked living at the camp.

"It wasn't bad. I got to where I kind of liked it. There was a bathroom, mess hall, a store to go and get your tobacco, your mail, and everything right there. If you didn't like it, it was just you."

The remains of the Hollis CCC camp on Highway 7 are now a preserved historical site with signs and markers describing the buildings mentioned by Mr. Dickson. We pass the deserted camp every time we go to the cabin, and I had often wondered what it was like when it was operational. I stopped one day to walk around and read the markers. One of the signs tells of the typical Hollis enrollee:

"Most of the enrollees were from rural farms within a fifty mile radius. Some families owned their farms, but many more were sharecroppers. The average young man had less than an eighth grade education. On most farms, school took a backseat to getting a crop in or out of the field."

The Encyclopedia of Arkansas History and Culture describes the camps:

"A brainchild of newly elected President Franklin Delano Roosevelt, the Civilian Conservation Corps (CCC) began in 1933 with two purposes: to provide outdoor employment to Depression-idled young men and to accomplish badly needed work in the protection, improvement, and development of the country's natural resources. Camps housing 200 men each were established in every state, from 1933 to 1942. During this period, 106 camps were located in Arkansas.

"CCC workers performed over 100 types of work, from planting trees to building parks to developing hiking trails. They also built bridges, some of which can still be seen along Scenic Highway 7. After nine years and three million enrollees, the CCC was dissolved by Congress in 1942, with many of those still enrolled entering World War II. More than 200,000 Arkansas natives had served in camps from coast to coast."3

After he fulfilled his enrollment at the CCC camp, Perk went on to work on the project to build the Nimrod Dam which was built in 1942 to control the Fouche LaFave river. It is a 3550 acre lake constructed by the United States Army Corp of Engineers.

Having worked and lived in Hollis so long, Perk is naturally very familiar with the area, and I asked him what he knew about our property.

He said the name for our mountain, Stover Shack Ridge, came about this way:

"There used to be an old house, an old man batched it over there; they called it Stover Ridge. Used to be a little old shack, kind of like Hatfield's down there. It was just a place to lay down, probably a fireplace or something to cook by. Right in there somewheres near the pond."

I have looked for remains of a shack near the pond on the road to the cabin, but haven't found anything. Nature has cleverly disguised any evidence of a cabin and buried its remains in a shallow grave.

The couple who beat back the beast of nature and built a cabin on our mountain were named Johnny and Janice Whitcomb. The cabin is made of white oak and cedar, and it has a steep roof, heavy wooden home made doors, and a ladder that leads to a sleeping loft. Because of its condition, we have tossed around the idea of tearing it down, but I don't want to destroy a piece of history. It is weather beaten and looks forlorn with its broken out windows and missing shingles, but it is dear to me, a constant that is always there, just like my beloved Forked Mountain.

When I sit on one of our plethora of huge rocks, I daydream about what it may have been like for those who have come to this place before me. Those struggled with these rocks, gazed at these mountains and stars, and prayed to the same God as I do when I am here.

We spend many nights at the cabin, and get up early to go to work back in Mountain Valley. One cold morning we got up to feed the animals before daylight. I wondered if Johnny and Janice had ever had a morning like this.

Stover Shack Ridge

The frosty, full moon morning,
silvery against the gun-metal gray barn,
dawns quietly as
towering, leafless silhouettes stand

at crooked attention

saluting

Orion, the Winter Maker.

A farmer, his breath fogging in rhythmic clouds,

shakes out hay for his little fuzzy coated herd

and they softly bleat their approval.

Inside the nearby cabin,

the specter rises from her sleep

and lights a lamp with shivery fingers

as her ghostly husband

opens the creaking potbelly stove and

blows his icy breath

on the coals.

The sagging chimney begins to exhale

as the day awakens.

My Neighbor's Flowers

The sun shone brightly the Sunday afternoon Danny
and I, along with daughter Ashley, her husband, Jeremy,
and baby Micah went to Charlie May Simon's home place.
We parked on the side of Rocky Crossing Road and walked
through the fallen leaves and briar bushes to the place
where two mounds of rocks that had once been fireplaces
lay covered in leaves and moss. A large flat rock capped
the idle well. There was a bit of chill in the February day,
just cool enough for a light jacket. This is my favorite kind
of weather - warm enough to be pleasant, but no danger of
chiggers or snakes.

As I stood in the pines that had grown tall in the
spot where the house had once stood, my mind saw a
determined young woman, bound to live without the
comforts of city life, smart, independent, and adventurous.
I saw her standing in this patch of woods, one hand on her
hip, one on her mouth in a thoughtful stance, imagining
what her cabin would look like and planning how she
would accomplish her project. She had on pants. Most

women in that era wore dresses, but not this one. She was willing and able to pick up an ax or a hoe and get with it. She also had the sensitivity to appreciate the delicate flora and fauna that quietly lived around her.

I saw her through the window as she sat and wrote in a notebook by the light of a coal oil lamp. She smiled as she wrote of the neighbors who had become her friends and as she devised the plot of the first book she would pen during her years at Rocky Crossing. Her arms are tanned and the veins in the back of the hand holding the pen look full and plump. Her nails are short and clean and her eyes are quick with intelligence and soft with the compassion and understanding that it took to make a life among the inhabitants of Hollis, and to be accepted as one of them.

The sound of the metal detector and soft laughing interrupted my thoughts. Danny and and Jeremy were digging excitedly, hoping to find a meaningful memento from our old neighbor's place. I sat nearby with eight month old, Micah, and let him kick and crumple the crunchy leaves.

They turned up rusty nails and cans while I used a small shovel to dig up some jonquil bulbs that were poking their new leaves out of the ground. I wanted to transplant them to our yard at the cabin so I would have a living connection to this lady I had only heard about, this writer who had lived here, maybe even had sat in this very spot, planting these bulbs. As I placed the bulbs into a basket, I thought of the similarities between my long gone neighbor and the neighbor Charlie May Simon had described in her book, *Straw in the Sun*, in which she tells of happening upon an old home place in the woods while looking for plants for her own house. She imagined what the woman must have looked like and retraced the steps that had beaten out the still visible trail from the house to the spring and felt the presence of the spirit of the one who had once lived there. She silently apologized to her ghost neighbor for each plant she took, but felt she did no real wrong in taking them because the lilacs and jonquils and burning bushes' real owner was the earth that sustained them.

Now, as I dig these bulbs, I like to think they may be the very offspring of the ones Ms. Simon dug over eighty years ago and moved to her cabin.

Thank you, Charlie May, for the flowers.

The Early Settlers

Prior to white men settling the area around Hollis, its human occupants consisted of various tribes of Native Americans. One of the tribes that inhabited the area was the Caddo.

Diana Angelo, archaeologist with the United States Forest Service, states, "The biggest use we had on the South Fourche LaFave River was prior to tribes during the archaic period up until about two thousand five hundred years ago. That was before pottery, so a lot of stone tools are at the sites. The first named groups, about a thousand years ago, would be the Caddo in this area. We can tell by their pottery."

The Caddo didn't have written language, but of course there are hieroglyphics. I had heard that there were Indian writings on the overhang near the gate to the road leading to the waterfall at Forked Mountain, and I asked Ms. Angelo about it.

"I haven't found any; I've looked," said Ms. Angelo. "But they did camp there. It is a site, and it's really hard to protect because people camp there and dig." She went on to explain that especially in earlier times, the Native Americans used outhangings as shelters with barely more than a wall behind them. Later, though, they used the caves that were abundant, especially in northern Arkansas. She said that areas along riverbanks are good places to look for artifacts, especially where a tributary joins a river.

The Caddo, who were the predominant tribe in Perry County, grew beans, corn, pumpkins, squash, watermelons, sunflowers and tobacco. They hunted small animals and gathered shellfish, nuts, berries, seeds, and roots. They made elaborately decorated pottery vessels, but Ms. Angelo said that it is rare to find an intact piece of pottery due to the acidic soil in the area which deteriorates the pottery.

The Caddo decorated their bodies with painting and tattooing, and women sometimes decorated their faces, arms, and torsos with elaborate designs. They wore their hair long and braided or tied close to their head while men commonly had short hair with a long braided lock.

The Caddo faced many obstacles which eventually displaced them from the area. Epidemic diseases, competition and hostilities with the Osage, Cherokee, and

Chocktaw, and westward spread of American settlement encroached on their domain. The last of the Ouachita Valley Caddo communities moved shortly after 1700. 4

Forked Mountain

The Native Americans who lived in the mountainous area around Hollis were no doubt as in awe of a 300 million year old icon that resides in the Flatside Wilderness area as people are today. The legendary Forked Mountain rises 1,234 feet amid the Ouachita Mountains, and its distinct appearance sets it apart from the surrounding ridges and hills. Resembling a dormant volcano with two peaks, one higher than the other, Forked Mountain is a regal monarch that presides over her wild kingdom with quiet magnificence.

Pronounced Fork-ed Mountain by the locals, the landmark has inspired awe, art, and even an Indian legend. Sandra Long and Marcus Phillips retell the story in the *Indian Folklore Atlas of Hot Springs National Park.*

"Once in the valley of Manataka, a lovely maiden from the south caught the eye of a brave warrior from the north. Even though their tribes were different, the two seemed to belong together. He was tall and straight and strong; she, gentle and loving as well as beautiful. When they looked into each other's eyes, they felt as though their spirits were joined and could never more be parted. But her father was a powerful chief who could not think of giving his daughter to a stranger who would take her away. As the days passed, the two lovers grew closer and closer. They spent all their time together, bathing in the magic waters, gathering healing herbs and berries in the forest, fishing in the streams, and sitting by the campfires at night.

"When her jealous father saw them so much together, he could not accept the thought that they might be joined forever and vowed to separate them. He could not kill the young lover or make war on his tribe because they were in the Valley of Peace where the Great Spirit had decreed that no blood should be spilled. Therefore, he called his people together and prepared them to leave the very next day.

"That morning when the chief had made ready to leave the valley he found his daughter missing. In a great fury, he took his strongest men and flew in pursuit of the couple, following their tracks up the trail to the north until he came upon their horses at the foot of the mountain. When he looked high up to the top, he saw the lovers asleep in each others arms under a rocky shelter. Remembering his vow to separate them, the angry chief called upon the Great Spirit to help him.

"There was a great clash of thunder, and a lightning bolt split the mountain at its summit. The two young lovers disappeared, but the Great Spirit took pity on their love. The maiden's spirit remained in one peak, and the brave's took its place in the other, forever joined at the base."

It's no wonder that the mountain has inspired legends and folklore. Its appearance just begs one to stop and stare and wonder. Forked Mountain has starred in a PBS special with Chuck Dovish and is probably one of the most photographed mountains in Arkansas. It appears in many of the illustrations by Howard Simon in Charlie May's books.

The mountain seems to evoke spiritual feelings. Comments I have read from those who have climbed to the peak mention a sense of spiritual quietude and an ability to relate to their predecessors who blazed the trail ahead of them. One blogger said he could now understand why the area was named Valley of the Vapors after witnessing the fog roll through the valleys as it does on many mornings.

At the base of Forked Mountain is a waterfall about twelve feet high that spills into a blue green pool. Nearby rock formations invite the adventurous to climb up to enjoy a peaceful view.

One late spring day, a group of us made our way down the old road bed leading to the falls. It cannot be reached by car, so we walked in sets of two or three, talking and laughing quietly. We were going to a baptizing. The pool at the falls seemed a perfect natural setting to observe this rite for our young people ready to solidify and proclaim their faith. The mood was subdued with the reverence of the occasion. There would be no splashing about and playing today. We took our places around the rocky bank as Danny and his brother Tony waded out into the waist deep water.

One by one the Christians who were declaring their faith and obedience to God carefully traversed the slick stones on the bottom of the creek.

"Father, thank you for Amy. We ask you to bless her and we baptize her in the name of the Father, the Son, and the Holy Spirit."

They lowered her into the cool water and raised her to her feet again. As the water coursed off her hair and face, she closed her eyes, consumed by the moment. She became weak, and her uncles helped her sit down in the shallow water near the edge. Two of the nearby women waded over to steady her.

The men continued this deeply moving ritual until all were baptized while falls splashed in the background and the trees stretched to reach one another high over the pool and locked their fingers together, forming a protective canopy over us, just as the wings of the Most High protect and shield us. The rock bluffs around us bore witness to the occasion, and I prayed that these who had signed their covenant with God on this day would be as immovable as these bluffs are.

Lookout Point

Danny and I drove along the dead end road past our driveway, and as we meandered along, we watched out the windows of the truck to catch glimpses of water snaking through the ravine below us. The leaves had fallen off the trees for the season, leaving them shivering in the cold, and the sky was gray and dull.

Danny found a spot to pull over, and we got out. He has a pretty good sense of direction and, as usual, took the lead as we walked through the pines and oaks. I zipped my coat, shoved my hands in my pockets and followed along. We walked downhill, stepping over fallen trees, and our jeans turned back the briars and undergrowth that grew out of the thick carpet of leaves and pine needles. We stopped when we neared a steep drop off and looked up and down the river. Danny said, "Let's walk on over there," pointing to an outcropping of rock.

I held onto little bushes as we descended. There were rock cliffs on both sides of us, and I, not being very adventuresome, especially where heights are concerned, was very cautious. We made it out to the point, though, and our reward was what some have called the best view in Perry County. To our right, upstream, we could see the river curving toward us in its relentless, persistent mission to dig through the earth, one pebble at a time, and carve its way ever deeper into the canyon. It had already done an admirable job, as evidenced by the bluffs that flanked it. The bluff on the right was much more pronounced, and the left side sloped off gently before rising again to another mountain.

When we looked to our left, a multicolored expanse led our eyes to the blue mountains beyond the valley. The resolute river plowed along below us on its way to join other waters in a great reunion before being raptured in droplets for the millionth time to the skies.

We sat down and talked quietly, amazed by the nature surrounding us. It was a place we wanted to share.

Lookout Point

The shady road to Lookout Point winds through my woods
like a good storyteller
in no hurry to reach the end.

I rest on the roadside and watch myself walk by,
first with a handsome man pointing out things about our
life together
and things we pass along the way,
like how easy it is to kick the little stones out of our path.

Next, I am with a gangly group of teenagers-
flirty, eye batting girls, who succumb to fits of giggles
while
the young studs swagger and guffaw
their way to the Point.

The laughter fades as we round the curve
and I look back up the winding road.
I am joined by a seven year old boy

with blond hair and sad eyes

who speaks of God and

the end of the world,

and of beating the fastest boy in the second grade.

After they pass, I come along with a friend and

we are immersed in conversation about

the kinds of things only women acknowledge and

understand,

like the feeling of being dissatisfied

when everything is wonderful,

and longing for something more,

and not knowing what that something is.

I get up from my rest and fall in behind my parade of

memories and

walk on toward the Point.

Sitting on the outcropping, Handsome and I marvel

at how the river below has cut through

generations of rock,

and even now

is chipping

away

at time,

our time,

our generation,

like sand through an hour glass,

and I wonder how many grains are left.

I arrive with the teenagers.

The daring young boys scale the rock formations and

heave rocks to the river and below,

laughing loudly in their almost-man voices

because they know they are

tempting Fate

and winning.

The boy and I drift in as the

group of teens dissipates

like the mist rising from the depths below.

I study the gray eyes that have seen too much

and the thin shoulders that strain under the load

he carries.

We snap twigs in our fingers

and he speaks raspy, knowing words

that belie his years,
and he asks me when I think
God will come back.

I look over my shoulder and watch
as my friend and I
come down the hill and assume
a good lookout point.
Silent tears fall and trickle down the
rock face
to join the river
as I listen
to secrets long held before they too,
fade from sight.

Today my only companions don't speak, laugh, marvel, or
confess.
They just lie there panting
as I lie back on my hand-pillow.

My hair, soft against my fingers, is still dark,
but the strands of gray remind me
of my own October.

I ask questions of the brooding sky,

but there is only silence.

Neil Thomas, Basket Tramp

Several years ago, I noticed a laminated copy of a newspaper article hanging on the side of the Coke box at Connie's store. It told of the Basket Tramps who had lived for a while at Hollis. As I read the article and looked at the pictures, I realized that the men had lived on our very property.

When we were cleaning up the old cabin, we found scores of empty cans of Bugler tobacco. There were Mason jars of canned meat, organic gardening magazines, a non-working propane refrigerator, and in the yard, the remains of a clay oven and a chicken coop. There was also an area where someone had stacked long heavy stones in a foundation pattern with the remains of a fence, presumably a garden spot, where they might have brought in soil. Large pieces of carpet covered muddy places. A broken down van and an International Travelall also decorated the yard, and it suddenly made sense where these items had come from.

The article, from a 1995 edition of a Memphis

newspaper called "The Commercial Appeal," outlined how the three friends wound up in Hollis Arkansas. I read it and took pictures so I could transcribe it and even offered to buy it from Connie, but she understandably declined my offer.

It wasn't until I began to research for *Living at Hollis* that I learned that one of the Basket Tramps, Neil Thomas, still lived in Hot Springs. I was delighted to find him, and we talked on the phone about his experience living at Hollis. I asked him how they came to live on 'my' mountain.

"Well, Michael, Ron, and I had left a religious commune in northern Michigan. We were shut down for building code violations, and we basically were wandering; we didn't know where we were going or what we were doing.

"We had those llamas, which was a silly situation, and I'm almost embarrassed to say it. We had been made homeless when we lost our home in Michigan, and we were very resentful. We had no real plans, didn't know what we were going to do. What we wanted to do was train the llamas to pack and walk across country in protest of our situation. Of course it didn't take us very long to realize how silly of an idea that was.

"But here we were in Hollis, camping right on the creek and we had been walking the llamas; I had sewn packs for them, and we had trained them to carry a lot of weight. It had been raining and raining, and there was mud everywhere, so these llama prints were all over in the mud. Well, it just happened to be deer hunting season. I think it was Berl Hawks who had tracked what he thought was going to be the biggest buck he had ever seen.

"He came upon us, these three people camping in a van, sitting on a stump, weaving baskets, with these llamas. I don't think he or anyone else really knew how to take us, but we were just ourselves, and we were friendly to people. We made coffee and got to know a lot of the locals, and we stayed for a long time (on the river) then someone offered us a bus that they had to camp in, an old school bus. It was January and it was cold. We started asking around and someone eventually put us in touch with Janice Whitcomb and Gene Reeves. We hit if off with them real nicely. They were such nice people, and we just moved up there on top of the mountain.

"We started gardening, tore up the ground with a pickaxe; we had tomatoes, corn, and vegetables, chickens, rabbits..."

I asked if they had built the chicken coop on wheels that still rests on the hill.

"No, Janice's first husband built that. It's a chicken tractor. You can move it around the yard and put a little pen around it, and the chickens will eat all the bugs.

"It was nice living up there; it was kind of like the Foxfire books. We didn't have any bills, no neighbors, no problems with the world. We were just able to stay up all night canning peaches and making leather and venison jerky. It was wonderful. It was actually one of the best times of my life. It was like an episode of "Grizzly Adams" or "Little House on the Prairie." You can see off to Forked Mountain from up there, and sometimes the clouds are lower than you are. It's just beautiful.

"But it was hard living up there, too. Anytime we needed to get groceries or any little thing, we had to drive out of that road. It was almost impossible sometimes to get in and out. One time we had a dead battery, and I ended up carrying that battery all the way to Hollis. That was crazy."

Neil was referring to the driveway to the cabin. The south side of the mountain is incredibly rough and steep. Bedrock keeps machinery from being able to smooth the road without hauling in a lot of gravel, and the rains wash out huge ruts in the road. One of my least favorite parts of this trek was the side to side motion of the truck that banged my head against the side window of the truck. We bumped and scratched up the old driveway for several years, which added to the remote feeling, but Danny finally made a new road on the north side. It is no superhighway, but it is better.

Neil continued his revery.

"Michael got snake bit one time. He was a stone carver. He was sitting under the cedar tree out in front of the cabin. He was carving a piece of stone and a copperhead fell out of the cedar tree and hit him on the arm on the way down. I think it probably only got one fang in."

Connie Hawks recalls that Ron had walked to the store for help. She went back with him and ice for Michael, but he decided against going to the hospital. The nearest hospital to Hollis is in Hot Springs or Danville, both about forty five minutes away, which is one of the disadvantages of living at Hollis.

The Bear

As I thought about snakes and other wild animals I had seen, I told Neil about the bears we had encountered because I wondered if they had had any experiences with them.

I told him about my brush with a blackie.

Danny and I had set up a motion activated game camera near a corn feeder to see if we were attracting any good sized bucks. We checked the memory card regularly and usually only saw does and turkeys. One day, though, we were surprised to see a big black animal in the pictures. A bear.

The bears had found the corn and discovered all they had to do was show up to get a free meal.

One afternoon as we walked down the hill to check the feeder and the camera, we heard something scratching and clawing its way quickly down a tree. A black bear hit the ground running. Bears will usually run when confronted by a human if they have a chance.

We decided to try to observe the bears in real life without scaring them away.

Danny had a ladder stand set up nearby. We walked down toward the feeder together, I climbed the stand, hauled up my still camera and video camera, and my pistol, and Danny walked out. Now bears can't count, and I'm sure the one watching from the woods thought someone had just come and gone and didn't realize one of us was still there.

I sat there ten or fifteen minutes, and I heard footsteps approaching. Soon a bear came into view and my heart pounded as I watched him come near. He lazily crunched the corn, sitting down at times. I was very quiet so as not to run him off.

I decided to try to take his picture. I slowly raised the camera, focused, and snapped a shot. I half expected him to bolt when he heard the shutter, but he didn't react at all, just kept chewing. I took several more pictures, and he never once looked up to find the sound. Okay, maybe video.

I started the camera and filmed him moseying around, totally unconcerned.

When he came close to the bottom of my ladder, I got a bit nervous. What if he suddenly looked up, noticed the paparazzi invading his privacy, and decided to teach me a lesson? I looked at my 9mm laying on the bench next to me and wondered if it was really capable of killing a bear. I had my doubts.

Here I was in a tree with a bear at my feet, and Danny was a good way off. I wasn't even sure if he was within earshot. As I tried to come up with a plan if the bear started an ascent, he moved away.

Good bear.

I had grown a little tired of sitting there, and I had plenty of pictures. I wanted to go, and I kind of needed to pee. I thought I'd just scare him away so I could climb down.

I clapped my hands and shouted at him. Nothing. Stood up and waved. Nada. Maybe I had myself a deaf bear here.

Now what was I going to do? I wasn't brave enough to just climb down. I was trapped.

I tried banging with a stick on the metal of the ladder stand. No response.

I shouted, "Hey you dumb ass bear! Get outta here!"

Crunch, crunch.

I put my hands on my hips, frowned, and tapped my foot. Decisive action must be taken. I had to get down one way or another.

I gathered my goods and my courage and started down the ladder. I eased down slowly with one eye on the bear at all times. My 9mm was in my belt, and I was prepared to make a hasty scramble back up the ladder if he suddenly turned vicious.

My foot cautiously searched for the next rung as descended with trembly legs and sweaty palms. When I reached about the halfway point, he *finally* caught sight or smell of me and scooted off through the woods. Whew!

When I was back on good old terra firma, I felt relieved and a little triumphant. I pinched the front of my shirt and pulled it back and forth to fan myself and evaporate a little sweat as I sauntered back to the cabin with some good pictures and a good story.

Neil remembered his run-in with a bear. "There was a fire pit area under some oak trees, and I had a stone and clay bread oven that I had built out there so I could cook outside and not have to heat up the house. We had been cooking something in that oven, and we were barbecuing too. Later I was in the house cleaning up, and I looked out the window over the sink and there was a bear behind the fire pit. And I went out there and yelled, and it took off, ran off." His must have had better hearing than mine.

Neil had an interesting story of an owl.

"We had a black cat named Rasta, and that cat would lay up on the peak of the roof at night to stay cool. We heard something that sounded like a cat coming from the yard. Our cat, who was in the house at the moment, started getting anxious, so we went out there to see what it was. It was a gigantic owl at the top of a dead tree. To us it seemed like it was disguising its voice to sound like a cat. Eventually that cat got picked off the top of that roof by something. I don't know what, but it was probably that owl. That was scary. I didn't know an owl could change its voice and I might have just been imagining it, but that sure was what it seemed like."

The cabin that the Basket Tramps lived in has a steep pitched roof with a high peak. The cat must have thought it was safe being that high, but predators are sneaky.

We have a fire pit somewhere near where the Basket Tramps had theirs. We moved several large rocks to sit on around a ring of smaller rocks that make the fire pit. As most people know, rocks are a great hiding place and favorite hang out for snakes.

One day we were sitting around the campfire, and my daughter Emily said, "Mom, don't move. There's a snake crawling out from under your rock." My rock was named Turtle Rock because it was shaped like and had naturally carved markings like a turtle shell.

I sat frozen, daring not to look down. I knew I'd better decide something quickly. With all the awe inspiring agility I could muster in my forty year old self, I jumped up on top of the rock. Emily said later that it had its head and about six inches of its body raised off the ground. I was wondering how I would escape my predicament when it slid back under the rock. Danny tried to make it come out so he could introduce it to the hoe, but it could not be persuaded. I think about that every time I sit on that rock.

We often see snakes, and not just in warm weather.

Danny and I were burning the remnants of a shed one cold rainy day. He turned over an old board to reveal two thick copperheads curled up for the winter. He poked at them with his rake, but they were sluggish with the cold, so he just picked them up with the tines of his garden rake and threw them on the fire.

While the Basket Tramps loved living on the mountain, snakes and all, it was difficult to make a living just selling baskets. Neil had learned to basket weave as a teenager and had taught Ron and Michael how to make baskets at the commune. They had no problem selling their crafts in the North, but it was different when they came to the South. He said they couldn't sell anything in Little Rock or Eureka Springs, but the people in Hollis were different.

"I don't know why they loved our baskets so much," Neil said. "I think the reason was that we were living a lifestyle that those older people there grew up with. We were just tracking rabbits and killing chickens and doing the things that they maybe longed for and they looked at like an idyllic life that they had way back when. I think that's why they liked us so much."

I think he hit the nail on the head with this assumption. I know hearing the stories of how it used to be in Hollis makes me long for a simpler time and our little piece of land and cabin without electricity helps me create the illusion that we are insulated from the unpleasant reality of the state of the world. I guess it's not really an illusion, though. When I am there, I feel safe and set apart. Like Aubrey Ballew said, "We're our own little world."

Because they had no electricity when they lived in

the cabin and I know first hand how hot it is in the middle of the brutal Arkansas summers, I asked Neil how they managed the heat.

"At one point we had a little twelve volt fan hooked up to a car battery, but mostly we got up early, did our work and then either walked down to the creek or just lay out under the cedar tree and poured water over us. It was hard. It was hot. But I was used to living without electricity or running water, so I was used to roughing it. I was young when I lived up there, and the heat didn't bother me like it does now."

They also had to hand draw the water out of the well.

"We watered the whole garden from that well. The llamas aren't really from this climate and we had to wet them down five or six times a day so the evaporation would keep them cool. I was always pulling water out of that well. I had muscles like you wouldn't believe. I must have hauled fifty or sixty five gallon buckets up a day."

Neil had to adjust a bit to living in rural Arkansas, especially to people's dialect and their way of phrasing things.

"I grew up in the North. We didn't keep cattle. Once

Berl Hawks asked me to come help him on his ranch because he needed to separate the cows. In my mind being young and never having been around cows, I thought he had a bull and he was mating a cow and they were stuck, like dogs get stuck.

"So we drive out in this pen, and he tells me, 'Get out of the truck and run around this way and cows are going to be coming through here' and this and that. I must have helped him thirty or forty minutes, and when it was over, I said, 'Where are the cows that we're going to separate?'"

The task was already complete.

"I didn't get it. I didn't understand what he meant. He made fun of me about that! He had only meant he wanted to separate one group of cows from another.

"I had a hard time understanding them. The way some of the people talked up there was a lot different than what I was used to.

"I remember Berl said he was building something out of tubafores, and I thought he was talking about an instrument like a gramophone or something. I had no idea he was talking about a two by four."

Neil concluded with this: "I've lived in a lot of places

all over the country – Northwest, Southwest, Pennsylvania, Tennessee – Hollis, Arkansas, is by far one of the most beautiful places I have ever been. And those people are the friendliest, most sincere people I have ever encountered, ever, anywhere."

Hiking

I like the solitude that the forest provides. The Ouachita National Forest sprawls some twenty seven hundred square miles and our place is in the middle of it, so I like to think of myself as the owner of the whole thing. I have learned to love hiking and exploring and I usually go alone.

Several years ago Danny and the kids and I had hiked down to the river out the ridge from the cabin, and I wanted to find that spot again.

I carry a fanny pack stocked with my .380, extra bullets, matches, Kleenex, a whistle in case I fall and need to call for help, and a can of pepper spray that swings from a hook on the pack as I walk along. I used to carry tampons but hallelujah for the hysterectomy.

Another important item I carry is a roll of yellow surveyor's tape to mark trails with. It keeps me from getting lost. At least that's the plan.

One late fall day I set out to find the hole of water on the river. I had tried a couple of trails in the preceding weeks but didn't find it. This day I would try another. I started off down the old logging road and it ran out after about a half a mile. I stopped and looked around, but there were only woods in all directions, so I tied a ribbon on a limb and kept going downhill. I figured when I reached the bottom there should be water. Every so often I'd tie a ribbon on a tree and look back to see if I could see the previous one.

Finally, I got to the bottom of the valley and stepped onto another old logging road, mostly grown up. It was more like just a trail. I looked left and right and decided to go to the right. I walked on. There is something about exploring that is a little scary. You want to keep going, excited about the possibility of what may be around the next corner, but you're a bit apprehensive at the same time.

I heard water and craned my neck to see. In a few more steps, the river came into view. It was flowing over some rocks and I looked upstream to find a gorgeous, still pool. My heart pumped with excitement, and I picked up my pace and trod along the trail, stepping over logs and wads of leaves.

I kept going along the bank and reached a nice spot

to survey the hole of dark green water. It was about two hundred yards long and fifty or sixty yards wide. Trees leaned over the water, gazing at their reflections like Narcissus. I could smell the creek water – a kind of muddy, dank, fishy odor – a smell that was affectionately familiar to me that made me think of the long, happy hours spent on the creek on the farm where I grew up.

I looked upstream where the water leapfrogged over stones and playfully jumped into the pool. It swam along until it reached the other end where it bumped and giggled into the next long hole.

I was delighted. I chided myself for not bringing a camera, but this gave me an excuse to come back, to take pictures.

This is when I noticed it was getting a little late. It would take me at least an hour to get back to the cabin, and it was all uphill.

I looked at the sky and estimated I had about two hours until dark. Better get going.

I took off back along the riverside trail, retracing my steps and watching for my flags. I found the spot where I came in from the woods and started the climb. I followed the yellow flags, but as the daylight faded, they became a little harder to see. I had to stop and look carefully for the next one. The exertion (and slight anxiety) was making me hot, so I took off my jacket. I tied it around my waist like I had done on the playground in grade school.

As I found each consecutive flag, I tied another in between so the next time I came down here I wouldn't have this problem. I was relieved when I reached the spot where the first trail had run out and I had started marking. It was all good from here.

Danny fussed at me a little when I got back, rightfully so, I guess. He made me start carrying a hand-held ham radio when I hike; we have a base unit at the cabin. He also makes me take the dogs. I guess he figures they will be like Lassie if I ever get lost or hurt, they will go back to the cabin and fetch him and lead him back to me while barking heroically and waving their flowing tails in the wind.

The Cabin

We bought our place at Hollis in 1999. Our children were still at home; Adam was fifteen, Ashley was thirteen, and Emily was six.

As mentioned, the driveway was a bit rough, but we managed to haul the materials up the mountain to build our little house.

When I say rough, let me explain what I mean by rough. Rocks the size of dishwashers litter the mountainside. Anytime we dig, it is likely that one or more of these rocks will be unearthed. Sometimes it is a refrigerator sized one. Rocks are everywhere.

Rainwater cuts ruts in the driveway, leaving deep gulleys. A road that has had no attention from grooming machines, such as road graders, is like a man who hasn't visited the barber in several years – that kind of rough.

There were places in the driveway that were washed out a bit at the time but not impassable. We bought a used Chevy Blazer to go back and forth to the cabin. One afternoon I picked the girls up at school and headed up to

Hollis to meet Danny, who was already there. We slowly climbed the rocky road. All at once, we heard a ppssshhhh sound. Flat tire.

We got out and dubiously studied the flat and discussed what we should do. There was nothing to do but climb on up and tell Dad.

Well, this was when I was a tad overweight, not just a tad, A TAD.

We started up the hill, and I quickly was out of breath. I had to climb ten or fifteen steep steps and stop to rest. Ashley made it to the top long before I did. She told me later that it really worried her how much of a toll it took on me to climb that hill.

Good ole Dad fixed the flat and drove the Blazer to the top of the mountain.

Several years later, when I decided to drop the pounds, I got to where I could climb that dang hill without stopping.

As we looked for a spot for the new cabin, we decided the first builders had chosen pretty well, and we picked a spot close to the one the Whitcombs had built. Theirs was pretty much uninhabitable. It has had its share of punishment with the weather and wind and has become home to scorpions, rats, snakes, and a few birds. We have, however used it as a shelter for Danny's deer hunting friends.

One night Danny's cousin Brent and his son Shawn slept in the loft of the old cabin. Brent said he woke up and felt something crawling on him. He violently shook his foot and sent a mouse sailing into the wall.

He laughed about it, but it would have been quite unfunny if it had happened to me.

Danny has been involved in construction all his life and he designed the small cabin to utilize the space as well as he could. Its one bedroom houses four bunk beds and a chest of drawers. The bathroom has a shower, commode, water heater in a closet, and a sink. Danny enlisted the help of family and friends, and the little twenty four by thirty six house went up. As I have mentioned, there was no access to electricity. We called the power company for an estimate to have electricity run up to us. Twenty-five thousand dollars. Well, that was a little pricey for us, so Danny began to research solar power and other alternative energy ideas. He educated himself and we bought solar panels, batteries, an inverter, and a whole wall full of stuff that I don't know anything about. He has insured that we have electricity for lights and small appliances, a propane water heater and cook stove, DC powered refrigerator and freezer, a solar powered pump for the well, and a wood burning heater. He is studying how to rig up an air conditioner. This will make me very happy.

Once we got the house built, we installed the cabinets that Danny built in his cabinet shop. We bought furniture and rugs at thrift stores and yard sales and installed lots of windows so we could enjoy the view of Forked Mountain.

We have several nieces and nephews of all ages who are frequent visitors to the cabin. One of the things they like to do at night is go out onto the deck to look at the stars. When you look down in the valley toward Trail 86, which is a gravel road, you can see the dim lights of the farmhouses. The kids were curious about the lights and asked us what they were.

Well, sometimes I find it hard to resist pulling someone's leg, so I made up a story. Danny picked up on the prank, and we wove the tale together.

"That's the ghost of Old Man Stover," I said.

"It is?" Amber asked, her eyes wide in the darkness.

She scooted closer to her cousin Emily. They were both in the first grade.

"Yeah. Haven't we told you about Old Man Stover?"

She shook her head and bit her fingernails.

"Well, you know the old cabin over there? That's where he used to live. At night he would go coon hunting with his lantern and ax. That was before flashlights, you know.

"One night he was off down in those woods down there," Danny said, and pointed to the lights in the valley. The kids looked where he pointed.

"Yeah," I said. "One night he went hunting and fell on his ax. Killed him. Now his ghost wanders the woods at night carrying the lantern. That's what those lights are you see down there."

"Huh uh!" Amber said.

"Really?" Jonny, who was a couple of years younger, asked.

"Did he really die?"

"That's what I heard. I'm not sure if it's true," I said.

Danny said, "Oh yeah, it's true. I've seen him lots of times."

Amber, who has been known to choke people in her

fright when she grips her arms around someone's neck, began to fret. "Does he ever come up here? Do you think he'll get me?"

"No, Amber, we're just kidding." I can never carry the joke too far. I start feeling sorry for the victim of the spoof. I told her the lights were from houses of people who lived in the valley.

She stared at the lights, not sure if she believed the first story or the second.

We went inside and started turning down the beds for the night, brushing teeth, and changing into pajamas. Everybody felt safe in the cabin, away from the lights.

Amber is now twenty years old. She says, "Y'all scared me to death with Old Man Stover!" and laughs about it. Oh well, she has a story to tell. Maybe she'll pull one over on her kids one starry night when we're looking down in the valley and see the 'lantern' lights.

One night, though, we had an experience with lights that was no made up ghost story.

It was hot. The sky was clear, and the stars were bright. It was dark but not really late yet. Danny had pulled some lumber up on a trailer behind his truck and unloaded it, so we were lying on the empty trailer, stargazing. Jonny, who was now about ten, was on the trailer with me and Danny, and Emily and Amber were on the deck behind the house.

Ashley had a summer job car hopping at Sonic. I got up to go in the house to call and see if she had made it home from work.

I looked down the driveway, which is several hundred feet long, and at the tree line just above the treetops there was a glowing orb. My first thought was a forest fire. But there was no smoke, no fire was in the trees below the ball. I shouted at Danny and Jonny. They jumped up and looked.

"What is that?" one of them said.

"I don't know!" I answered.

I stared at the light, trying to figure it out. I had a video camera in the house, and I started in to get it as Danny hollered at the girls to look.

About that time the ball moved away from us down the mountain; we could still see it through the trees as it departed. I didn't have time to photograph it.

Amber and Emily ran over to us, but it was gone. It remains an unsolved mystery, but it is something that Danny, Jonny and I will never forget. A UFO? Swamp gas?

Certainly no helicopter or airplane. No flashlight or lantern. Maybe that's what we get for scaring little kids.

Campouts

When Ashley and her husband Jeremy were in college and they and their "neighbs," (neighbors who were also fellow students) needed a getaway. A weekend long 'campout' provided an escape. It has become an annual event, and we usually have a theme for the party. One year it was Pioneer Days.

The women had planned a craft project, and we gathered around the island to make bonnets. Mona, our daughter-in-law's mom, had brought scads of old fashioned looking material, a cardboard pattern, hot glue guns, and scissors. Now all we had to do was use our imagination. Each of the girls fashioned a bonnet while we laughed, alternately making fun of and complimenting each other's creations.

Outside the men held an archery contest. They sported various lengths of beards they had grown for the "Best Mountainman Beard" competition. The best archer won a bag of beef jerky wrapped in brown paper tied with string.

Desserts made from treasured recipes adorned the table, numbered so everyone could vote for their favorite.

After the women finished their bonnets, the men gave audience while we paraded across the deck to their applause. We in turn clapped and cat called while they displayed their manly beards. Jeremy, my son-in-law, had bought a huge fake black beard that reached the middle of his chest. This won him first place, hands down. He was awarded a straw hat and corn cob pipe.

Lindsey, one of the neighbs, won the bonnet contest, and she donned the vintage full length apron she won. Ashley borrowed Jeremy's beard, and they posed for some hilarious pictures.

Abby Friddle won a dutch oven cookbook for the "best dessert" prize for a wonderful, gooey chocolate oatmeal thingy, which I had to have the recipe for. It was delicious.

Another year we had a pet costume contest. Between members of the family, we had a bunch of dogs we had gotten at the pound, and we dressed them up in cute little outfits. Festus, a terrier mix, wore a straw hat, vest, and pistol; Chester, a Shitzu wannabe, was dressed as a pirate; Harley, a feisty brown guy with a black muzzle, was a prisoner with black and white stripes. His sister Dixie had learned lots of clever tricks and she and her 'mommy' Betsy showed out for us.

We once had a variety show, which included singing and playing guitars, juggling, and storytelling. We had rigged up a small amplifier with a microphone, but we had a little trouble with wind noise. The wind is almost always blowing on top of that hill.

Everyone brings lawn chairs, and we stretch hammocks for naps and entertaining displays of balance. We usually hike somewhere, sometimes to the Forked Mountain waterfall, to Lookout Point, or through the woods past the barn down to a pond near the road coming in to the cabin. No matter which way we go, we always have to climb back up.

We spend a lot of time eating. One of the dishes that has become a must have is our version of succotash. I have a huge iron skillet about fifteen inches in diameter, and we cut up onions, green, red, and orange bell pepper, okra, yellow squash, zucchini, corn, and chicken, and cook the conglomeration on the fire pit. Emily usually makes her own big skillet of fried potatoes. There is nothing like the taste of food cooked outside while you're talking to your friends and choking on eye burning smoke.

We also always have a big breakfast on Saturday morning with turkey or deer sausage, bacon, a huge pan of biscuits, gravy, hash browns, cinnamon rolls, coffee, and orange juice. Lunch is usually hamburgers and hot dogs, chicken strips, brats, (the sausage, not the kids), steaks, veggies, or whatever else people want to throw on the grill.

On the last campout my dad attended, he and Adam fried fish. My dad loved to fish, and he loved to cook them, too. I hope he has found some great streams in heaven. At times when I watch the sun set and I am missing him, I think how nice it would be to join him, how easy and joyful it would be to glide through the clouds and enter into peace, but I have responsibilities here.

To My Dad

The sun turned over and pulled up the covers,
letting through only enough light
to pinken the veil
between you and me.
Oh, to slip through the clingy, orange and gold
shadowy billows!
To spring into flight, weightless, powerful,
and surge toward the departing rays!
Your smile beckons me to everlasting peace,
and yet,
I look back.

A baby is smiling at me
with a sweet, gummy grin
in a mouth that has not learned to bite
or hurt.

A little girl with wispy brown curls,
clasps her little pink-nailed hands,
tightly shruggs her shoulders

and bends forward
in a fit of giggles.

A trusting toddler with heavenly blue eyes
waddles to me with his little arms outstretched
in an innocent, irresistible gesture.

A proud, pretty widow with a rabbit head cane
is holding onto my arm
for support
and company.

A daughter who once pretended to marry her Papa
whispers of her prince and white dresses.

Her sister, my confidant, is serene and
sings of why and how
and of
the masks people wear.

And their brother,
my first,

whose milky breath I still remember,

curls his adult body in my lap and says

"I love you, Mommy."

And,

The man who is my

Forever,

They will not let me go.

When we started the campouts, the kids were young, but now they are all married and most have babies. In 2012, we had our first campout with kiddos. Ellie brought her battery powered Jeep. She chauffeured the other kids around the yard, one at a time. Levi, Ellie's younger brother, was content to let his sister do the driving (besides being not quite old enough,) and observe most of the activities from a safe vantage point. He is like me in that he is a bit cautious. We are the ones who hang back and make sure no one gets killed riding a roller coaster or swinging from a rope into the creek before we decide we *might* try it. Levi and I have a special friendship, one I like to think is similar to the one Danny and his grandmother shared. He calls me Nanny, and much to my delight and Danny's angst, he prefers me to his Papa.

When the sun started going down that Saturday night, the campers scattered tents around the yard and everyone got settled. They turned off the lanterns and flashlights as the sky became inky black. The October night proved a little chilly for Ashley and four month old Micah, though, and they abandoned their tent and came in the cabin about midnight. He was wrapped up like a little papoose, but his face was cold. Ashley climbed up into a top bunk and I lifted him up to her, trying (pretty unsuccessfully,) not to wake everybody up. As I was raising him up, I caught a whiff of something. I whispered, "I think he pooped," which made everybody in the dark bedroom crack up.

While Ashley changed the baby's diaper, I tiptoed into the kitchen to get a bottle. Since the kitchen and living room are the same room, I tried not to wake the people who were sleeping there.

"How's Micah?" asked Daniel from the darkness. I rolled my eyes at myself, silly to have thought they could possibly be asleep after Ashley creaking open the storm door when she came in and the giggling from the bedroom.

"He's fine," I said quietly. I don't know why it seems like you have to speak quietly just because it's dark. Everyone was wide awake. I turned on the propane wall heater, padded back to the bedroom and handed up the warm bottle. I got back in my bunk, cold from the chore.

I could hear Micah drinking his bottle and the breathing of the sleepers in our room becoming steady as they were lulled back to sleep. I could tell Ashley wasn't asleep, though. I could feel her tension as she worried about Micah being cold, from trying to sleep in an unfamiliar bed, and from just being too tired to sleep. She was thinking; I knew she was. Ashley has always turned things over in her mind and thoroughly inspected them, sometimes putting things on glass slides and examining them with the microscope of meticulous contemplation, a tedious habit, maybe, but she finds things others miss.

Just Us

When all the campers were gone, trash picked up, and dishes all washed, we settled back into our old routine. Happily, Danny said, "I like it the best when it's just me and you."

He and I rearranged our living room in the cabin for the winter. We pulled two recliners near the wood burning heater and we spend many evenings talking and eating popcorn or drinking coffee.

We plan what we're going to do for the next project on the place or talk about Mary Ann and Wanda, Laverne and Shirley, Thelma and Louise, Pez, Skittles, Sugar Baby and Maggie, who are our goats. We recently were blessed with a squirming litter of ten puppies from our dogs Scout and Jem, who were named after characters in my favorite book, *To Kill a Mockingbird*. Scout and Jem are livestock guardian dogs. They protect the goats and live in the barn and fields with the herd.

We talk about things that have happened to us at the cabin - of puppies, kids, bears, people we used to know, people we still know, the state of the world and our place in it, and many other things that have happened in our thirty plus years of marriage as we warm our feet by the stove and sip our decaf.

Sometimes we recollect what it was like when we were children. Danny adored his grandmother, who lived near him when he was a boy. He has told me many times how he loved to spend the night with her and the foods she fixed for him and how she never spoke ill of anyone. He has an endearing reverence for her, and he says she was one of the best women who ever lived. He still misses her, though she has been dead many years.

Grandma Ellen

She still stood straight, even after many years of carrying
burdens.
A boy, tentative and bold at the same time,
followed her
to the barn,
where Tom and Dimple waited for their mistress
to serve them.

As she prepared the grainy meal,
an unfortunate mouse attempted to
partake of the portion reserved
for her faithful.

She seized a nearby weapon and
in one fell swoop,
killed the vermin
with a teacup.

In the house where chickens pecked under the floor,
they ate sliced hamburger fried in an iron skillet

and his favorite –
homemade biscuits with
pure white sugar –
his bread of life.

He lay on the feather bed and
closed one eye
to catch a glimpse of a bright star
through a crack in the ceiling near the wall.

Special effort had to be made
to see the beautiful star,
not everyone could,
but he was not everyone.

He blinked heavily and
turned his gaze on the old granny
sitting in the next room in an old rugged chair.
She braided her hair and twisted it into a
crown around her head.

Now, when he lies in his bed
with a crackling fire in the nearby wood stove,

both eyes are open
as he waits for the
Bright Morning star
and for her.

Ellie Drives the Truck

"Papa, when we get on the dirt road, can I drive?" asked Ellie from her car seat.

"Okay," he said.

Kids learning to drive on dirt roads in Arkansas is a time honored tradition. I remember when I was six or seven that we had to take our trash to a landfill which was several miles from our home. My dad let me sit in his lap and steer our old truck when we had to go to the dump. Our old Chevrolet had metal cattle guards on the bed and a clutch. First I had to master the steering, like Ellie was doing.

The tires crunched on the gravel as we turned off the highway going to the cabin.

"Okay, let me out!" Ellie said.

We stopped on the road and I got out to unstrap Ellie. She crawled over the seat onto her grinning Papa's lap. He put the truck in gear.

As we drove along he said to her, "Ellie, are you driving?"

"Mmmhmm."

She chattered unintelligibly as she turned the wheel more than was necessary.

"Hey, keep it in the road!"

Amazingly she adjusted and straightened her course. She watched the road for as long as her three year old attention would let her.

"Look at dem flowers back der," she said as she pointed behind us. I cackled as Danny quickly steered us away from the ditch. We carried on like this, heading for first one ditch and then the other, for the two miles or so on the road to the cabin. About halfway up the driveway, Danny has a permanent wooden tower stand for deer hunting. Any tower to Ellie is for Rapunzel, from the Disney movie, "Tangled." I always have trouble remembering the name of the show; I want to call it Twisted, but that wouldn't be a good name for a kids' movie.

She waves her short dark curls around, pretending she has long blond flowing locks like 'Punzel's'. Danny loves to tease her about Eugene, the handsome young man who rescues Rapunzel from the tower.

"Hey, Ellie, you oughta climb up in that tower and

let Eugene come up there and kiss you."

"No!" she protests, but I think secretly she thinks this would be fun.

As we climbed the hill, she noticed the sign we had recently nailed to a big oak tree: "Danger- Guard Dogs on Duty." I read it to her as she requested.

"Eww, dog on doodie. Gwossy." Yes, the English language is confusing. Duty and doodie are pronounced the same with amusing results.

Right after we passed an old shed that she likes to think is the residence of a spooky old man, she noticed a bucket on the side of the road.

"Hey, what's that?"

"Your Granny done that," said Danny. "She put a bucket on the side of the road and just left it there."

"Gwanny, you ought to know better than that! Why did you do that?"

"Well," I stammered, feeling silly and awkward being called on the carpet by a toddler, "I had some rocks in that bucket in the back of my car. It had kind of a round bottom on it and it was tipping and rattling in there, so I stopped and emptied it out, and left it there. I need to pick it up."

"Yeah!" she agreed, as she chauffeured us along.

Danny laughed with amused affection. We reached the top and drove along the ridge to the cabin. The goats and pony trotted ahead of us, a hungry welcoming committee. As Ellie and I got out to open the gate, Scout and Jem ran out, tails wagging, which sent Ellie to squealing and climbing me. She likes dogs, but not their face licking and big whacking tails. It's safer a little higher up.

The Goats

Having domesticated animals in the middle of the
Ouachita National Forest brings to them an inherent risk.
Wild animals are certainly prevalent in the woods around
our place. Coyotes circle around at night, howling with a
cacophony that will raise the hair on your neck. It is a
bizarre, unsettling sound that at times seems too close for
comfort. They present no danger to humans but goats are
another story. Coyotes will make a quick meal of an
unattended goat. That's where the dogs come in.

This winter, our nanny goat, Pez, was the first of the
season to give birth. Newborn goats are at risk not only to
fall prey to predators, but also to the cold.

Danny had gone out to check the animals and found
the little billy goat half frozen, abandoned, in the barn. He
brought the droopy baby in the house and said, "We've got
to warm him up."

I ran the sink full of warm water and put him in. I
had to hold his little head out of the water, for he just
didn't have the strength to do it himself. Every so often, he

would bleat loudly, which I took as an encouraging sign. We got him out after a few minutes of soaking and vigorously towel dried him, then turned on the blow dryer. He continued to just lie there, but he was breathing and his eyes were open.

Danny milked his indifferent mother and we squirted milk in his mouth with a dropper. We continued this every thirty minutes or so while he rested by the wood heater. Occasionally he kicked his feet in a swimming motion and lifted his head.

That afternoon Emily arrived from college for the weekend. She, being my sensitive child, immediately assumed care of the little goat who she named Oliver, after Oliver Twist, because he had been abandoned. She fed him and held him and talked to him, encouraging him to live.

I had to return home that evening and left the goat with Emily and her dad at the cabin for the night.

They all three came home the next morning and Em said she had kept up the feedings all night and was exhausted. I wrapped Oliver in a towel, put him in a laundry basket, and relieved her so she could take a nap.

I dropped milk onto his tongue every so often, but he was growing weaker.

Being a nurse, I have often heard the rattly breathing that indicates approaching death. Poor little Oliver was succumbing.

Emily's bedroom door creaked open and she emerged with wild hair and a pale face. In the nasal tone of one who has just woken up, she asked, "How's Oliver?" as she rubbed her face and went to the baby.

I told her, "Honey, he may not make it." I pointed out his irregular breathing and open mouth. He didn't swallow when we put milk on his tongue.

She, in her tired state, and stressed from college, began to cry. She had worked so hard. She said, "Isn't there anything else we can do? Take him to the vet?"

I said, "Well, sometimes babies just die. They don't all make it." It is a hard fact of farm life. Practicality has to rule. He was a male goat, one that we probably wouldn't have kept anyway. It wasn't prudent to spend money on him. Emily didn't want to hear this and thought me insensitive.

It took her a little while to absorb this reality but she realized my rationale when she thought about it. It is just her nature to mother things, and I wouldn't have her any other way. At least Oliver didn't die alone.

Homer Wells

Mr. Homer Wells is a ninety-year-old resident of
Hollis. He and I visited for about half a day, and he told me
a good deal about the ins and outs of the area, whilst
smoking cigarettes and drinking Coca Cola. I noticed that
he had red stains on his boots and backs of his hands, as
well as a few patches of the same color on his shirt and
overalls. I wondered about this and finally was able to
work it into the conversation and asked him about it.

"Oh, I been paintin'. I had me some turning plows
and I decided to paint them up and maybe sell 'em." He
told me about his work as a heavy equipment operator, a
logger, and about the time he spent sailing on the Great
Lakes. He sat in a well worn recliner near a large window
and kept watch on the occasional vehicles that passed,
absently flicking ashes into a deep green colored glass
ashtray.

He relaxed as we talked and bent over to loosen his
boots and slip them off. He crossed his white socked feet in
the low window sill and opened another Coke as he spoke

of the great flood of 1927.

"I was just five years old, but I remember the water was way up. Dad had the fields plowed up, ready to plant. It washed it down to the clay; you could see where the plow had cut it. It took years to get it back.

"This flood we had in 1982, oh Lord, it topped that one. Way up there, way bigger. A lot of this highway you couldn't travel. Lord, yes, you could see it right yonder." He pointed to a group of buildings several hundred feet away. "My brother lost forty-two head of cattle."

He told me about that night.

"I go to bed early. I knowed it was a rainin' and about ten o'clock, he called me. He said, 'Our cows is drownded.' I got up, he might have come over here. See, he could hear his'n a bawlin'. I went to drivin' the roads, and at 2:00 o'clock that morning, I had to quit. It drowned me out, done blocked the road. My cows had all come to a hill next to the barn, though, they was safe."

Homer said that he found his neighbor's cow about three miles downstream after the flood, trapped in a bunch of briars. She was the only one of his they found alive.

Turning to a different subject, we talked of his life as a young man in Hollis.

"Back in my time, if you went to Plainview, (a small town near Hollis) you was goin' sommers. I was over there every Saturday night through the winter, showing out."

I asked how he showed out.

"Using the bottle. When I was sailing on the Great Lakes, we'd run over one another when we'd get ashore. Up in Minnesota, it wouldn't be but about two, two and a half hours (that they were on shore). If we did any drinking, we had to hurry and do it. Course, I drunk my part through the winter. I was making pretty good money, uh huh. I drank a little of that home made stuff, but it was too rough."

I said, "I've heard that was pretty stout."

"Damn right, it's stout. I usually bought bonded whiskey (bought at a store). I spent a lot of money on it. Back then twenty dollars was hard to come by. It was in the forties, one, two, three, uh huh," he said. "This was before I was married." I asked about his wife.

"I went with my woman about four year, and I went with a girl up there in Chicago for Lord, four or five year. My wife was from Plainview. I don't remember exactly how I met her, at a dance probably."

"Did you like to dance?"

"Nah," he said, waving the question away. He just went to dances for the company. "Hell, when yer drinkin', ya gotta have a crowd."

We laughed and moved on to other things. Homer told me his memories of having to log around various graves that were not located in cemeteries. One girl of about eighteen died when there was three feet of snow on the ground, and she could not be taken to a doctor or one come to her. She was buried on her father's place. Another man, Daniel Nooner, had a grave in the woods and had requested to be buried standing up. Mr. Wells knew exactly where this grave was located, and I asked him to tell me where it was.

"You couldn't find it," he said. "I could show you, though."

He called his son who lived across the street.

"I'm goin' out for a while. This old gal wants to see that grave over at Marble Hill, and I'm gonna take her to it. If we're not back in an hour, send a posse." I laughed when I overheard this and he smiled, pleased to have made a funny.

He pulled on his boots and tightened the laces.

"Now, let me go to the bathroom; I'll be right back."

He disappeared into the back part of the house. When he returned, he was pulling on an insulated flannel shirt with a rip in the sleeve that showed the cotton stuffing. "If you need to go, it's right back there," he said, motioning to where he had come out.

I went into the bathroom. The door was propped open and looked like it hadn't been closed in a long time. I looked around and debated whether to close it, but since he was in the kitchen and I planned on making it quick, I left it open.

When I came back to the living room he had on his cap, standing there waiting for me.

"I just leave that door open all the time," he told me. "I got up one night to go to the bathroom and the door was open about halfway and I ran into it. Blacked both my eyes. Now I just leave it propped open."

"I want to show you something," he said as he went to the window sill behind his recliner. He handed me a black, heavy ball about the size of a softball. What was it? I first thought it was lead, maybe a cannon ball. It was pitted and not perfectly round. I could tell it wasn't machine made.

"Know what that is?" he asked.

"No. Is it a cannon ball?" I asked, wondering if any Civil War skirmishes had occurred around here.

"No, it's a grinding ball. I found it in the creek. It's Indian."

"Oh! That's really cool."

I later asked an expert on Native American artifacts about the ball. He said that because it was round, it was more likely a game ball. Grinding stones were more oblong to fit easily into the hand. Diana Angelo, the archaeologist from the Forest Service, agreed. Whatever it was, it was a treasure, a treasure Mr. Wells was saving for his grandson.

"Do you mind if I smoke in your car?" he asked.

No one had ever smoked in my car, but I said "No, it's fine." I could always air it out and use some Febreeze. After all, he was humoring my curiosity. Soon we were touring the dirt roads.

"Slow down right up here, Hon." We topped a hill and I stopped the car. He pointed out to another hill through the woods. "It's right out there."

I saw yellow and white markings on trees, and I asked him if he minded if I walked out to it.

"OK," he said. "Now I can't walk with you; I'll just wait here," he said as he lit up.

I walked down a steep slope and back up the next hill. A weathered tombstone with a barely decipherable inscription read: 'Daniel Nooner,' and there was a newer headstone in front of and below the old one that read: 'Daniel Nooner, born 1799, died 1870.' Research of genealogy records revealed he died of "consumption," the old term for tuberculosis. I snapped a few pictures wondering why Daniel Nooner had been buried all alone in the woods and why he would want to be buried standing up? Of course, it probably wasn't woods when he died. Given the hilltop location, it may have been a pretty spot in a field on his farm. I could only speculate.

I got back in the car as Homer was finishing his cigarette, and he tossed the butt out the window. He pointed out other graveyards as we went by. We drove past Dry Fork Cemetery and Hames Cemetery on our way toward Road Forty Five. We forded shallow creeks and went over concrete slabs in creek bottoms as he told me of the people who used to live and farm in the area.

"This used to be all fields; it's all grown up now." There were woods on both sides of the road with remnants of fencing and old sheds and barns that were barely able to stand due to the frailty that comes with age. They bravely hold onto the trees that have rudely grown through their floors and out their roofs, and pieces of them fall away every day as they gradually lose their battle with gravity and time.

Many farmers gave up their lands and moved to cities when it proved too difficult to make a go of farming. People wanted to work at jobs that were not so labor intensive and they could actually make money, not just grow the crops and animals they needed to simply survive. Now, the abandoned farms bore witness to how thoroughly Mother Nature reclaims what is borrowed from her.

We rode in silence for a while. I asked Homer if he went to school out here when he was a kid.

"I went by it," he said with a mischievous smile.

"There was a school up here at Avie (Ava.)"

He showed me the location of the school as we drove by on the way back to his house. He recalled a special teacher named Mr. Cox.

"In my schooling, one teacher was the one I done most of my learning from. Cox was his name. He was raised right up here. He just had a way of telling you, a feeling, a something, that it'd soak in. Course, I was just like all the other kids, meaner 'n hell, I guess." Homer recalled another teacher whom he admired.

"One of my teachers up here, he hurt his ankle, God, it was that big (made a circle with his hands around his ankle,) black as it could be. Now he walked and didn't miss a day of school teachin'. He had to walk, but he didn't miss a day, just a hobblin' along. Hawk was his name."

Mr. Hawk had exemplified determination and dedication to Homer Wells. Persevering with an injury, fulfilling his duty even with an obstacle, spoke more about character than any lecture. Sometimes school lessons are wordless.

Donald and Jane Crain

Our closest neighbors in Hollis are the Crains. They own the place at the foot of our mountain on South Fourche. Although the Crains and we bought our places at the same time, in 1999, I had never been to their cabin.

I crossed the slab over the creek bed in about six inches of water, topped the hill, and turned into their driveway. Donald had said the gate would be open, and it was. I wound through the trees down a gravel lane, and soon the red roofed cabin and surrounding buildings came into view. The river rushed in the background as I parked next to the shed covering their firewood. A playhouse surrounded by swings and slides was next to the red roofed carport, and a bunkhouse was across the yard from the main house. The morning sun speckled the ground as it shone through the leaves that had refused to fall for the winter. The breeze was cool as I got out of the car, and it blew the scent of wood smoke from the chimney toward me. The scene was like something from a movie that you wished you had starred in or the picture in your mind when you dream of a perfect getaway.

A stone sidewalk led to the front porch, and as I made my way toward the house, I heard someone calling behind me. Donald smilingly welcomed me and we climbed the front steps, and he opened the door. Jane, a slim woman with short graying hair, wearing jeans and a faded denim shirt, stood next to a roaring fire in a wood stove. We sat down at an oak pedestal table with a cup of coffee, hazelnut decaf, and got to know each other.

Donald lived in Hollis and went to the Ark school through the third or fourth grade. His father taught there until he got a teaching position in Perry. Donald continued, however, to help his grandparents (Dennis and Lillie Crain, who owned the store and post office for several years) on their farm on weekends in the summer, days he remembered vividly.

"We raised truck patches. We raised so many peas we picked them in cotton sacks. I worked out there in them fields day and night. All we did was farmed and went to church." He spoke loudly with a voice that had come from years of teaching and coaching and had a robust laugh to go along with it.

He remembers hauling hay before tractors and hay

balers came along. I easily imagined him in the hay fields. Even now in his retirement, he was a healthy looking, tanned man who was dressed in denim overalls and a white cotton shirt. He spoke with the rapidity of someone who gets things done.

"We hauled loose hay, thousands and thousands of bales, the hardest work I've probably ever done. I was the one up in the barn 'cause I was just about twelve or thirteen years old. They just covered me up, wasps this close to my head, just thick.

"When Johnny Whitcomb or Mr. Bolander, one, came in here with a hay baler, I thought I'd died and gone to heaven."

They had a little trouble at first.

"You might have a bale eight foot long and weigh twelve pounds. You'd try to pick it up, and it'd just twist around, or it might be a foot long and weigh fifty. Then we'd get it adjusted finally - didn't matter how it was, I was tickled to death to have it, cause it beat hauling loose hay."

Loose hay hauling involved cutting the grass with a horse drawn mower and rake pulled by two horses. Donald had a team of one high spirited horse and one not so much.

"One time Grandpa put me raking hay, and I was

going along there raking hay, not paying any attention. Right along the edge there, a creek runs through, and it had washed out. There were some steep little old gullies, and that hay rake wheel just fit in that gulley. Well, I got down there and got stuck. Those two horses, they was sitting there, and I didn't know what to do, and all at once they started yanking, one of them wanting to run off, and I could hear that thing twisting and screeching, about to break in two. I said, 'I'm gonna have to go for it.'"

I pictured a young sweaty man trying to calm one horse and persuade the other to go.

"Well, I got out of there, but I know I stayed stuck down there a good thirty minutes trying to get out." He laughed at the memory.

After the hay was raked into rows, it had to be raked into piles to be pitchforked onto a wagon with frames on the side so it would hold more. One person would be on the wagon to stack.

"I was the stacker because I was too little to throw it up there. I walked around on it and stacked. My Uncle Harley is the one I worked with the most. He worked like a house on fire, never slowed down. When we started hauling hay bales, eventually, he never turned his truck off. He'd just start down through the field and leave his truck a runnin', throwing hay just as fast as he could. It may be bouncing, doing this and that, but he'd get it to the barn. It always would aggravate my grandpa because he liked to plod along and think things over and take his time. Uncle Harley'd come in a whistlin' and a runnin'. Grandpa'd just fuss about it. 'Confound, gonna tear something up!' He did tear some stuff up, but he got some stuff done 'cause he wanted to go fishing!" Donald slapped the table and laughed exuberantly.

"Anyway, he'd throw so much hay up in the barn, you couldn't see anything but my head. That's all I was doing, trying to keep my head out."

He said it was hot, dirty work.

"Oh, gosh, I spit up black stuff – there was so much dust in that hay. I know there was weeks I spit up black stuff, my lungs had to be full of it. Mmph." He looked like he was about to cough and spit just thinking about it.

"I swear I could do it today. I could shut my eyes and harness a mule. We always did it before daylight. We had them fed and us fed by daylight, and we were out going to work. We didn't have that much time off."

Donald's grandpa occasionally let him take off to go

fishing, a much needed break, no doubt. He reminisced about those days while Jane searched for a picture of their pet bobcat they had told me about since the cat is a little shy and wouldn't show herself. Jane showed me a copy of a Christmas card featuring their pet who had been abandoned by its mother under their deck. She is in a fighting stance about to square off with a big raccoon on their porch. What a perfect portrayal of life in the woods!

Fishing

Hollis provides plenty of streams, small lakes and of course, the South Fourche LaFave River to fish in, so fishing is a favorite pastime of many residents.

Danny recently bought Ellie a fishing pole and we took her and her daddy down to Cove Creek Lake. She and I walked along behind Daddy and Papa. Papa cast a jig into the still water below the dam and hooked a little bass right off.

"Hurry, Ellie, come reel him in!" She ran to grab the pole and reeled in a wiggling fish about ten inches long. She was proud, but not proud enough to stick her thumb in his mouth to pick him up. They caught a few small fish before Ellie decided she wanted to go for a ride in the canoe we had strapped to the roof of our Chevy Tracker.

The boys unstrapped the boat and slid it into the water while I fastened Ellie's life jacket. They boarded and pushed off. I walked along the bank taking pictures as they paddled and cast. She soon grew tired of this, too, and wanted to get out and walk with me. She came ashore and shed the life jacket. I pointed things out as we walked among the trees along the bank.

"This is a stick that a beaver has chewed all the bark off of." I handed her a stripped white stick about a foot long.

"There's a bigger one."

"I want that one, too." It was about five feet long and a couple of inches thick on the fat end.

"No, it's too big. Granny doesn't want to carry it."

"I want it."

"No, let's just take the little one. I don't want to carry that big one."

"I'll carry it," she said.

She picked up the big stick and managed to get it all the way back to the truck, whacking things along the way, including me. After all that effort, I had no choice but to let her bring it home.

As we drove up Rocky Crossing road, she leaned against me and fell asleep with her little fingers stained with Cheetos and her hair messy and wind blown. I wonder how much she will remember of her first fishing trip. I wonder if she dreamed of wiggly fish and beaver sticks and being paddled along in a boat in some of the prettiest country in the world, or of the two men who hooked fish for her and let her have the thrill of bringing them in, or of the grandmother who clucked about life jackets and dry feet, and who held her up when she had to use the bathroom.

My own grandmother wasn't the outdoors type, but even with the perpetually perfect hair and clothes, she indulged me and my sister. When Dad bought our farm when I was four, she rode our pony and petted our Collie dog, and even rode the tire swing just because we wanted her to. Suzanne and I always called her 'Grandmother,' the title she preferred, but when Danny and I had children, she became Granny King. Talk about loving the great grandkids! She was so proud of them. The look on her face and the tone in her voice when she introduced them to someone was priceless. Now that I am a Granny, I understand that a whole lot better.

Connie Hawks

I took a chair and cracked open my diet A&W root beer while Connie rang up the young couple who were wearing backpacks and motorcycle boots. I studied the shelves behind the counter while they paid for their Monster and Redbull and bananas. There was an old Mobil Gas sign near the cigarette rack, photographs of hunters in blaze orange with their bucks, decks of playing cards, Redman tobacco, hydrogen peroxide, turkey callers, Off, and ear plugs. On the counter there was a bucket of Double Bubble and a basket of some baby sized Moon Pies next to the lottery tickets.

An elderly patron in a white t-shirt and blue jeans with rolled up cuffs shuffled in on a cane. Connie greeted him by name. He said he wanted to pay his bill. She reached up on the shelf behind her and pulled down a plastic file box, flipped to his tickets, and pulled them out. She added them up on an adding machine, tore off the tape, and gave him the grand total: $79.42. He handed her four twenty dollar bills and said he had a low front tire.

"Okay, I'll have to go out there and turn on the compressor; there's something wrong with it, and I can't just leave it on." She banged out the screen door and he took a seat next to me.

"Boy, it's nice weather out there," I commented to him.

"Yep."

Connie came back in and sat down with us. They chatted about how everybody was while the compressor compressed.

"You reckon that thing's ready?" he asked.

"I imagine. I'll go do it for you," she offered. "Want me to gauge it?" She scurried behind the counter and started digging first in a pencil holder and then flipping through items on the shelves looking for the gauge.

"Well, I can't find the gauge. Somebody's took off with it."

"That's alright. You can tell when it's full," said the man with the gray five o'clock shadow.

Connie soon had the tire aired up, and he pulled himself out of the chair and tottered over to the candy rack. He tossed two Snickers bars on the counter along with a couple of one dollar bills, and she gave him back a few coins. I'm sure this guy could remember when candy bars were a whole lot less than a dollar.

As he left, a woman in a uniform came in. After you sit for a while, you can tell who's a local, and who's a passer through. She was a local.

"Connie, I guess I want a bologna sandwich. Hot cheese."

"Wheat or white?"

"Wheat."

She took the same seat the man had occupied, one down from me.

"Are you a nurse?" I asked while Connie made the sandwich.

"Yes. Home health."

"Oh, I'm a nurse, too," I told her.

We talked about various aspects of nursing, and she told me about her territory.

Connie appeared with the bologna sandwich, handed it to the nurse, and resumed her post behind the register.

"What were the cops doing here?" the nurse asked Connie.

"Oh, trying to serve a warrant." She said the man's name. "They can't find him. I told them he wouldn't answer the door. They're going to have to catch him driving down the road or something."

Three deputies had been in the store when I arrived. As the women talked, one of the officers came back in to let Connie know what had happened. He looked very professional in his brown pants, tan shirt, and neatly trimmed hair. He hitched his thumbs in his gun belt as he spoke.

"No luck," he said. "He might as well just give up and do his thirty days and be done with it." He shrugged his shoulders. "I guess we'll try again later."

He pushed open the screen and said over his shoulder, "You ladies have a good day."

The nurse was eating her sandwich. "You live around here?" she asked.

"Sort of," I said. I told her my name and a little about myself. Soon I mentioned my book project.

"Oh, you ought to talk to my mom. She's in her eighties but she's got all her wits. She's in the nursing home at Dardanelle, but she grew up here. Her name is Euleta Davis, but they call her Katherine at the home. She's pretty busy up there, being on the welcoming committee and everything."

I wrote down her name and number. Soon Diane had finished and had to go back to her rounds.

I asked Connie to share with me some of her memories about running the store. I asked if she had ever been scared.

"Well, I have not hardly ever been scared at the store. One time this man came in here; I was fixin' to close up that evenin," she trailed off.

"Were you in here by yourself?" I asked and she nodded.

"I shouldn't tell this. He started taking his pants off." Oh, no. I could see this getting bad, but it turned out to be someone who was unstable, not a rapist.

"I called the sheriff and they came out here. Scared me to death. They caught him just inside the Garland County line. He had run off, but they got him. He was mentally off. That was the time that I was scared the worst."

"You never have had anybody try to rob you, have you?"

"No. I had some people out here one day though, you know how they mill around, one would come in, and one would go out. I went out there and said, "Y'all haven't paid for the gas yet."

"He said, 'Oh, I'll come back in there and pay for it.'

"He come back in here, and he paid, and he put the change money in his shorts. He turned around and said, 'You didn't give me my money.'

"I said, 'Yes, I did, you put it in your shorts. You have your money.' He turned around and left. Afterward, I was scared, because you just don't know about some people."

The store has never been robbed but has been broken into three times. Mostly stolen were cigarettes. Once the thieves took enough time to open a box of garbage bags and filled them with loot. Twenty bags full of stolen merchandise.

"It was the same guy twice. He got arrested both times, but they never done nothing to him. You know that's what's disgusting."

"Well, tell me. What's your favorite thing about running the store?" I asked.

"People," she said. "I like people. I've met a lot of nice people. I've dealt with a lot of accidents, and people getting sick out here. This one time, this guy from

Louisiana came in here and he said, 'Would you call an ambulance?'

"I said,'Yeah, what's wrong?'

"He said, 'I just stopped over there on the mountain and gave CPR to my wife.'

"They were old. I called the ambulance, and they were there probably within fifteen or twenty minutes; they came in a hurry. They kind of thought it was a diabetic thing, 'cause she was diabetic. I asked the ambulance driver, 'Would you please just drive slow, so he can keep up with you?'

"Anyway, him and his daughter came back out here, probably a week or so later videoing and doing all this stuff, making pictures.

"The lady had had a heart attack, talking on the phone to her daughter in Denver. She had to have a five (vessel) bypass. They were so nice. They brought me a plant.

"I just meet a lot of nice people. I don't never have no problem with people coming through. Never have."

Danny and I have seen multiple motorcycle accidents on Highway 7. One afternoon we were going home from the cabin, and as we neared the highway, we saw flashing lights and several cars pulled over on the edge of the road. Lots of people were milling around. As we got closer, we could see the helicopter that had landed in the middle of the highway to airlift a motorcyclist who had had a wreck in the curve near the turnoff to the cabin. Unfortunately, the man died before he could be transported.

We have owned bikes ourselves over the years. Danny and our son Adam both had Honda Shadow 750's at one time, and they rode up and down Highway 7 quite a bit. One afternoon, they and Emily, our daughter, were out cruising. They pulled the bikes to the side of the road to take a break, thinking they were well off the road. As they were stretching their legs near the bikes, a car traveling south crossed the center line, forcing a northbound truck off the road straight toward my family. The truck slid on the loose gravel, and the driver fought to regain control while Danny, Adam, and Emily struggled to get out of the way. When the truck would veer left, they would jump right, when it would veer right, they jumped left. As the truck drew dangerously near, Danny shoved Emily as hard as he could out of the path of the truck just as it slid to a halt. They were all breathless including the driver.

Now jokingly they call the spot Squirrel Run, because they were darting one direction then the other, like a squirrel does when a car is bearing down on it.

Connie spoke of motorcycle accidents as well.

"One year our fire department went to twenty-two motorcycle wrecks, just in a short time. We've got our helicopter pad now which helps a lot. We have had to land up there at 210." She was talking about the same accident I described, near Forest Road 210, also known as Rocky Crossing. "They sat down on Bear Creek bridge one time to get a couple of them out."

A customer came in and Connie asked, "How are you?"

"Cain't tell," was the cheeky reply.

The River

Rivers are the lifeblood of many communities. An integral part of the development of Hollis was the Fourche LaFave (pronounced Foosh Lafay) river. South Fourche is a fork of the main river that flows through Hollis. It continues to play a large role in the area, providing a place to fish, camp, and swim, and it is watched carefully in heavy rains for flooding.

The origin of the river's name is open to debate: "fourche" is French for "fork," and "La Fave" may be in reference either to a family that once lived along the river or to an early settler, Peter La Fave. The South Fourche La Fave River rises in the Ouachita Mountains near Onyx in Yell County and empties into the Fourche La Fave River near Deberrie in Perry County.

"The Fourche La Fave River has been the site of human habitation since approximately 10,000 B.C. In the historic period, French explorers and trappers operated in the area. The river valley attracted early American settlement; Aaron Price, who reportedly was the first settler in Perry County, made his home along the river in 1808. Many early settlers grew cotton in the river bottoms.

"The river has historically been especially susceptible to flooding. One of the most noteworthy floods occurred in 1833. The Flood of 1927 also greatly impacted the river and surrounding areas. Nimrod Dam was begun in October 1938 and completed in 1942, however, the project did not stop all flooding along the river; one in 1982 proved quite damaging."5

The Flood

The flood of '82. It is a time that stands out in the minds of the people of Hollis. Connie remembered it well. "In '82, the river got up in the store. It got up over the spillway. Got in Harley Crain's chicken houses. They got us up at 3:00 in the morning and said, 'You might want to get up, that river's out here in your front yard.' We moved the cars out in the front, got them out of the way.

"Berl said, "Harley's the one that's in trouble.' He said, 'Let's go down there.' So we went down there. Them chickens was floating and cows was bawling. The cows came out down here at the bridge. I don't know how many cows they lost, I really don't remember.

"Their butane tank was floating and a spewing. It was pretty bad." Natural gas is not available in Hollis, so many people have capsule shaped two hundred and fifty gallon butane tanks to fuel their stoves, water heaters, furnaces, etc. They just rest on top of the ground or are lightly anchored so water can easily pick them up and move them.

"The road (Highway 7) was blocked. It was sloshing over this bridge." The bridge spanning the nearby South Fourche, is about twenty feet over the water during normal levels. "The water was over the road up here by the church," she said, speaking of the Pentecostal Church about a half mile north of the store.

The flood is well remembered by the residents of Hollis. Like a river our lives are sometimes placid and calm, other times the water moves along at a good clip but is manageable, and still other times are marked by high water and wind and 'floods' of events, and we feel out of control. Thankfully, though, I have my family, my 'trees,' to help me when I feel overwhelmed by life's torrents.

The Flood

I am the long green river pool,
still, save the occasional circles
of my inner fish
surfacing for air.

I lie back in my bed
and watch the panicked clouds
rumbling and tumbling, falling, stumbling...

My uninvited guest kicks down the door
and gushes through the rocks in my head.

Vainly, I try to contain the onslaught,
but I am losing my grip.
I desperately try to absorb the torrent,
but I am saturated.
I overflow into the trees that stand next to me
and seep into their roots and wet their ankles,
forcing them to wade through my mess.
The levees of self control and sensibility
have failed.

The surge loses its fury
and I am left weak, breathless.
The moss is rearranged,
the stones have tumbled and rolled,
fallen leaves have been washed back into their branches
into unnatural wads
and I am the color of watery brown cocoa.
My clarity is gone.

My steady course,
with its predictable turns,
gentle shoals,
and slow languid pools,
has forever changed
by this unwelcome outburst.

The trees, my precious trees,
stand beside me
with their intertwining roots
that run into me, through me,
they stand limb locked,
and they shall not be moved.

Euleta Davis

Mrs. Euleta Davis, resident of Dardanelle Nursing and Rehab Center, age 82.

Katherine, as everyone at the home calls her, sat in her room waiting for me the afternoon of our scheduled appointment. She had bright eyes and a friendly smile. Her hair was arranged attractively in a curly, casual style, not like that of an old lady.

"I'm Audrey Breshears," I said, and offered my hand. "Are you Mrs. Davis?"

"Yes," she said as she took it. Another lady sat in a wheelchair between the beds in the room. A TV was loudly making its presence known from the corner of the room.

Mrs. Davis bid me to sit down on her bed. I did, and we exchanged pleasantries.

"Would you like to go down to the lobby?" she asked. "It might be quieter."

"Sure," I said.

"I'll be back in a little while," she said to her roommate, who barely looked up from her magazine.

Mrs. Davis pushed herself in her wheelchair and said, "I can walk, I just have to have someone help me. They're afraid I might fall." She led me down the long hallway of the nursing home.

"Hey, I like your hair!" exclaimed one of the nurses.

"Thanks, Hon, I just got it done today."

"Well, it looks real nice."

With a smile lingering on her face, Mrs. Davis pushed on. We settled in a sitting area in a hallway where there wasn't too much traffic, and I pulled out my recorder.

"What was it like when you were a young woman?" I asked.

She told me she had grown up at nearby Cherry Hill and had married her husband when she was sixteen years old. They had two children, a son and a daughter.

"We lived in a log cabin at Hollis. We heated with wood, cooked with wood, too. I was married ten years before we got a butane tank. At one time, we had a kerosene cook stove."

I told her I had often wondered how the temperature was regulated on a wood cook stove.

"Well, some of the old cook stoves had a deal on

front, a monitor, that showed how hot it was. Now on top of the stove, you're just going to have to check your stuff, and if it goes to cooking too fast, you just scoot it back. Most of those stoves, the one that Mrs. Davis (her mother-in-law) had when we married, had a reservoir where the water would heat when you had the stove a goin', and there was a warmer above it that kept the food warm while you were cooking."

I commented that it must have made the house awfully hot, which reminded her about when she gave birth to her son.

"I had my son in June, and it was hot. The room I was in had the windows raised, but we didn't even have a fan or nothing. My mom and my husband's aunt and another woman was there besides the doctor, and my husband, and they just kept fanning me. It was a hundred and something degrees." She laughed a little, shaking her head.

"That wasn't so much the 'good old days' was it?" I asked.

"I say if we go back to the good old days, I sure couldn't handle it, not as old as I am now. I was used to the hot weather, working in the fields and stuff when I got married; I guess it didn't bother me. I didn't wear long sleeves, and that's why my arms look like they do." Her forearms had some age spots and a few bruises typical of ladies her age.

In fairly isolated communities like Hollis, independence and fortitude were a must. She told me of some of the ways they used what was available to them.

"If you had milk you wanted to keep cold, you had to put it down in the well. Sometimes you would put it in a lard tin with a lid on it. If you had it in one of them glass jugs, you had to be so careful when you went out there to draw it or you'd hit it on the inside of the well. It was rock. Then the bottle would break and you'd ruin your well water. I used to draw out Mr. Davis's milk glass, and he'd say, 'Now, girl, you be careful, don't you hit that jug.' I never did break one, but I was scared to death I would."

Of course there was no refrigeration, so the well was the coldest place to keep something from spoiling. "You just had to make do with what you had," she said.

"Do you ever remember a period of drought or hard times when the food supply got low?" I asked her.

"Oh, yeah. I remember back at home when the garden didn't grow too good. I remember one time that lasted five or six weeks when I was a kid that all we had was turnip greens and cornbread."

"Davis, you tellin' a big one?" A nurse was turning a lock to a door, letting herself into a break room.

"Yeah, I'm full of it!" She laughed good naturedly as the nurse disappeared behind the heavy door.

"I like turnip greens and cornbread, but..." I said.

"Yeah, but day after day of it," she trailed off, thinking about that.

"My mama would make a cake out of sorghum molasses. And cookies. She made cookies out of molasses. That's what we had for syrup. That was the best syrup you could have." It was made from sugar cane and processed near where she grew up.

"Did y'all grind your own flour and meal?"

"Back when I married my husband, they did over at Cherry Hill. My daddy would take corn to the grist mill.

"Need a little help?" Euleta spoke loudly to a man in a wheelchair who was causing a traffic jam. "Gonna make it, Daniel?"

"He's OK," said the woman who was needing to get by. The man continued his microsteps, pulling himself along with his feet. His mouth hung open, and he studied the floor as he inched by. The lady in the chair behind came up on his left, saw her opening, and made a pass in the straight stretch.

We continued our talk of grinding. "My son was about ten months old. On Saturdays, that's when Mr. Davis would grind the corn. The baby couldn't even talk, but he kept begging and begging. He wanted on that mule. His daddy took him over there and finally put him on the mule. He went around a time or two and he was satisfied.

"Course you did the same way when you made sorghum molasses, you took it to the sorghum mill to mash the sugar cane. We grew it at Cherry Hill. I planted it, plowed it, stripped it, and everything else, and my dad would haul it to the sorghum mill in the wagon. The grinding wheels mashed the liquid out of the sugar cane and it dripped into a pan that had one big compartment, and two smaller ones on each side. Somebody had to stand there as it was cooking and keep that foam off of it. It would cook down and get thick and they'd put it in glass jars. The man that owned the mill kept some for doing it and we got the rest."

"I like your hair," said a lady who had stopped to talk to Euleta.

I laughed and said, "You're sure getting a lot of compliments on your hair," I turned to the visitor. "Everyone who passes by says they like her hair."

"They should. You know our hair is our looks. When you fix your hair, you feel better, sometimes. Don't tell me it's no wonder I feel like I do because of the way my hair looks," she cast her eyes down.

"You look fine," Euleta said, convincingly. "You look *fine.*"

"Well, since they took my purse and all my money, I don't know if she'll fix my hair," said the lady. "She's as sweet as she can be; she went ahead and did my hair once, but you can't ask somebody to..."

Mrs. Davis said, "Well, you've probably got some money left in the kitty, don'tcha 'magine?"

"In the what?"

Euleta laughed a little. "The kitty. Your little bank account with Theresa?"

"I don't know. The bank account was completely moved." She was obviously speaking of a different account. "Our names aren't on the thing to sign," she spoke hesitantly, unsure.

"Well, I betcha Becky will fix it tomorrow," Euleta

said with a comforting smile.

"This is one time I hope you're right. Over me," the lady said and turned and shuffled on down the hallway.

As Mrs. Davis watched her walk away, she explained to me how the facility keeps spending money for the residents and that she was sure the lady who spoke with us could afford to have her hair done.

The overhead speaker interrupted our conversation. "Maintenance to wing three, maintenance."

I told her that when I left I had to meet Danny at the farm to give our dogs medicine for Tick Fever. They were taking a round of antibiotics that had to be administered twice a day.

She said, "You better be sure and watch the ticks on yourself. I tell you what I use for chiggers – vinegar."

"Does that work?"

"Yeah, I put it on my socks, shoes, britches legs, out pickin' berries."

"Boy, you can get loaded up picking berries," I said.

"It smells bad. That's why the chiggers don't like it, I guess. Avon – what was that?"

"Skin So Soft," I answered. "That didn't work so good for me."

As we discussed bug repellents, a woman in a housecoat with disheveled hair and a big knot on her forehead approached us. She took Mrs. Davis's hand, and Euleta called her by name and asked how she was.

"I'm okay. Have you got any openings down there where you are?"

"Well, no, I have a roommate, but you're just down the hall from me in the four hundred wing. I won't let anything happen to you. You just go on back down there and wait for them to cook supper. We'll eat supper and after supper I'll go back to my room and you'll go back to your room and we're gonna be just fine."

The lady with the pop knot smiled weakly. She nodded her head and told Mrs. Davis she liked her hair.

Katherine Euleta Davis seemed a little out of place here. She was an unexpected pleasure, like a bird that sings in the middle of the night, unaware or unconcerned about the darkness surrounding her. She had made her nest in the space allotted to her with the things she could reach and was quite content to gently twitter and chirp in a way that called the other birds to her, the birds who had broken wings or who were storm blown and disoriented, who were looking for their way home. Her song was beautiful, quietly sung, with a sprinkling of soft laughter to make it as comforting as a feather bed and a warm quilt on a cold night. She sang gently to those who would cock their heads and listen for a moment, for she was no hawking bluejay, no cackling crow. She warbled her notes in the shadows, singing only for those who were awake enough to hear.

The Early Days of Hollis

From the early 1800's to 1930's, row farming, or
planting of crops that grow in rows, like cotton, corn, oats,
wheat, and sweet potatoes was common in the area.
Natural disasters like floods, drought, insects, and
competition from big business farms in other states forced
many families to leave their Ouachita farms for industrial
jobs in cities.

The first permanent settlers in the Ouachita
Mountains, though, arrived in about 1803 with the area
being included in the Louisiana purchase. Most were from
other southern states further east like Tennessee and
Georgia and were of British descent. It took several years
of backbreaking work to tame the land. Large timber had
to be cleared, stumps removed, houses built, wells dug, and
fences built.

At the time of the Civil War, there were many good
farms, but there were very few slaves in the Ouachitas.
Most people in Perry County joined the Confederacy. After
the Civil War ended, more families moved to the area and

staked their claims. Homesteaded farms were typically a hundred and sixty acres.

"In 1862, the Homestead Act was passed and signed into law. The new law established a three-fold homestead acquisition process: filing an application, improving the land, and filing for deed of title. Any U.S. citizen or intended citizen who had never borne arms against the U.S. Government could file an application and lay claim to 160 acres of surveyed government land. For the next 5 years, the homesteader had to live on the land and improve it by building a 12-by-14 dwelling and growing crops. After 5 years, the homesteader could file for his patent (or deed of title) by submitting proof of residency and the required improvements to a local land office.

"Local land offices forwarded the paperwork to the General Land Office in Washington, DC, along with a final certificate of eligibility. The case file was examined, and valid claims were granted patent to the land free and clear, except for a small registration fee. Title could also be acquired after a 6-month residency and trivial improvements, provided the claimant paid the government $1.25 per acre. After the Civil War, Union soldiers could deduct the time they served from the residency requirements.

"Some land speculators took advantage of a legislative loophole caused when those drafting the law's language failed to specify whether the 12-by-14 dwelling was to be built in feet or inches. Others hired phony claimants or bought abandoned land. The General Land Office was underfunded and unable to hire a sufficient number of investigators for its widely scattered local offices. As a result, overworked and underpaid investigators were often susceptible to bribery."6

Dogtrot Houses

Most homesteaded farms were located along creeks. Creeks provided life blood to the farm, so a family likely used the location of a creek, among other things, to determine where they would settle. A convenient stream could provide a location to wash clothes, swim, fish, draw water to bathe, wash dishes, drink, cook, even baptize if it were called for.

The typical house built next to a creek was of the 'dog-run' or dog-trot style.

"A dogtrot house historically consisted of two log cabins connected by a breezeway or "dogtrot," all under a common roof. Typically one cabin was used for cooking and dining while the other was used as a private living space, such as a bedroom. The primary characteristics of a dogtrot house was that it is typically one or one and a half stories, having at least two rooms averaging between eighteen to twenty feet wide that each flank an open-ended central hall. Additional rooms usually take the form of semi-detached shed rooms, flanking the hall to the front or rear.

"The breezeway through the center of the house is a unique feature, with rooms of the house opening into the breezeway. The breezeway provided a cooler covered area for sitting. The combination of the breezeway and open windows in the rooms of the house created air currents which pulled cooler outside air into the living quarters efficiently in the pre-air conditioning era.

"Secondary characteristics of the dogtrot house include placement of the chimneys, staircases and porches. Chimneys were almost always located at each gable end of the house, with each serving one of the two main rooms. If the house was one and a half or the rarer two stories, the necessary staircase was usually at least partially enclosed or boxed-in. The stairway was most commonly placed in one or both of the main rooms, although it was sometimes placed in the open hallway. Although some houses had only the open central hall and flanking rooms, most dogtrots had full-width porches to the front and/or rear.7

Because of the air current created by the 'breezeway,' it was a common practice to drag pallets out to the area to sleep. Household tasks such as ironing were also done in the cooler area. Arkansas summers can be brutal, and the design of the dog-trot house was a clever way of dealing with it.

Danny constructed our barn in this fashion, with stalls on either side of the breezeway and a larger adjoining area for hay storage, lawn mower, tools, etc. It does have a breeze nearly all the time except on very still days.

The cabin, however, is just a rectangle, not designed with a breezeway, and on hot nights, we sometimes drag the bunk bed mattresses onto the deck so we can take full advantage of the moving air. When the moon is full, we can watch the goats meandering around, browsing, eating the brushy leaves and nibbling grass. The scene takes on a silvery cast, almost like a black and white photograph that is underexposed, too dark to make out all the details, but plain enough to know what's going on, like a veiled comment from a good friend.

Without the interference of city lights, we can make out many of the constellations. Orion is easy to see with his sparkling belt and sword, and the waves of the millions of tiny stars that make up the Milky Way stretch from one horizon to the other in a celestial blanket.

The year we built the barn, there was a bumper crop

of gnats that loved to fly into any available orifice on our faces. We had to wear caps with turkey hunter's netting to keep from ingesting them.

When summer had come and gone, we made a way to keep warm in the barn. We had a barrel with a pipe sticking through the roof as a makeshift fireplace to keep our deer hunting family members comfortable between shifts sitting on the deer stand. They had propane lanterns, lawn chairs, a coffee pot, and a Coleman stove- a regular little camp.

The barn has many uses. We have a goat milking stand in one of the stalls, and in another stall, Scout has her puppies. She is having a harder time keeping them corralled as they get bigger and start walking around. One we call Dirty Britches. He is white with a black mask, and grayish spots on his seat, which makes him look like he sat in something and got his white pants messed up. Another, Zip, is a pretty little girl with brown hair that has black tips and four white feet.

We keep feed for the dogs, horses and goats in metal trash cans with lids in the barn. We have to keep this behind a gate to keep all the over anxious helpers from assisting. The goats are like piranhas when it comes to sweet feed, and Rudy, the mule named for his rude personality, is not above nipping your hand or arm in his zeal for grain. Danny has a specific routine and order in which he carries out the feeding, and it confuses the animals if he doesn't do it the same way every time. I usually feed the dogs when I help, and I wait until the end, so everyone is in their stalls. Scout is skinny with gigantic udders from nursing ten puppies. Poor girl. She eats like a pig, but now the babies are getting where they crawl into her food bowl and eat that too! Kids.

More About Goats

The goats make a beeline for the horse stalls when Danny lets them out of the pen where they eat to see if there are any leftovers. Mary Ann is one of the more assertive ladies, and she has a stout head butt. I was watching the goats sniffing for spilled grain around the feeder when she slammed Shirley. I was in the path, and she cue balled me with Shirley into the corner pocket. I called her a few derogatory names as I got up and brushed off my jeans.

Goats, even though they can be annoying at times, are entertaining animals. The first goat of our current herd is Maggie. She is a Nigerian Dwarf with fuzzy gray fur and cute little horns. We got her when she was just a few months old and Jem and Scout were young, too.

She thought for a long time that she was a dog. She hung out with them under the porch, slept with them, and played with them. Her favorite trick was to jump from the overturned watering trough onto the low roof of the old cabin and run around all over the top of the building. She would go to the very top, run as fast as she could down the steep slope of the roof and dive off, landing perfectly. It was a hoot!

Thelma and Louise are named after the characters in the movie of the same name. If you have ever seen it, you know that the two run off after committing a crime and are on the run the whole movie. Well, when we first got this pair, we had unloaded them and were letting them get acclimated to the herd. Thelma, the taller, goofier one, took off down the driveway at a dead run, making her getaway, with Louise in tail. We finally persuaded them to come back with a feed bucket and the rest of the goats, but they earned their names well.

Last fall, when the girls were all feeling friendly and wanting some male company, we borrowed a Spanish billy goat from our neighbors, Cleto and Terry Mendez. Back in the summer the girls had decided to go exploring and had ended up at the Mendez farm down on Hwy 86. Terry, bless her heart, had penned up our roving herd until we could come get them. That's how we found out they had billy goats. They had a motley crew of three males – a Boer with a crippled front leg, a short, dark coated Pygmy, and a big hairy Spanish goat with huge, outward curving horns who caught Danny's eye. He thought of all our nannies at home, and he had matchmaking on his mind.

Cleto said we were welcome to borrow the big goat, so one October day we pulled the horse trailer down to the Mendez's. We had a real time catching the billy. Danny and I and Cleto's son, Izzy, spread out in the field trying to force the big goat into a corner so Cleto could lasso him. He ran all over the place, making sport of us. I think I heard him laugh once as he ran by me, shaking his huge horns and wagging his bearded chin. We finally chased him into the barn and slammed the door behind him and Cleto. I waited outside the barn, and when they emerged, the goat had a rope tied around the base of his horns with Cleto holding the other end. Cleto dragged the goat for a while then the goat drug Cleto for a while, but we eventually managed to load him in the trailer. When I say we, I mean they.

Back at the farm, we let the smelly fellow out to meet the girls. It was love at first sight for a couple of them. We dubbed him Speedy for obvious reasons.

We soon learned that he could jump like an Olympian. We had him in a round pen at first. It was made with metal horse panels about six feet tall. He could get a run and clear the top with ease, especially if the girls were going out to graze and he thought he was getting left behind. We soon gave up trying to keep him penned up and figured he wouldn't run off if his harem was with him. He spent most of the fall with us before we returned him to the Mendezes.

Buying Buck

Thanks to Speedy, we doubled our herd size when all the does had kidded, but as summer came around again, we searched for a billy goat to buy for the upcoming breeding season. Danny had been reading up on hardiness in goats, and wanted to add some Kiko blood to our goats. He scoured the internet for something he liked. I called a number he had found for a young Kiko buckling.

"Do you still have the goat you advertised on Craigslist?" I asked.

"Yeah, sure do," said the man on the other end. I had him on speakerphone so Danny could hear, too.

"Can you tell me a little about him?"

"Well, his daddy is one eighth Savannah, and seven eighths Kiko. Mama is full blooded Kiko."

Danny smiled. He said to me where the man couldn't hear, "Let's go see him."

I mouthed, "This afternoon?"

He nodded.

"Are y'all gonna be around this evening?" I asked.

192

"Yeah. What time?" he wanted to know.

I calculated quickly in my mind how long it would take to get to Northwest Arkansas and what we had to do that morning. "Around three?" He said that would be fine and gave me directions.

Danny and I love to go on goat buying trips. Seeing people's farms and talking with other goat farmers is always fun. They tend to like the same things, like alternative energy, homeschooling, dogs, and other farm animals, as we do. I also enjoy seeing their setups for fencing, milking, and grazing.

We passed the two old bulldozers the man had told me to watch for on the gravel road. They looked like they hadn't pushed any dirt in a good long while, like maybe in my lifetime. We spotted the gate and saw a little sedan behind a fence and a few goats, and a lady was walking toward us. She was a young Asian woman with a bright pink blouse, white shorts, knee high rubber boots with flowers on them, a white wide brimmed hat with a string tying it around her neck, and leather farm gloves on. She smiled and waved to us. As she walked toward us, it became bouncingly obvious that she had neglected to wear a certain undergarment.

I got out to open the gate and greeted her. As I swung the gate open, her husband, a white man of about forty five, dressed in gray jersey shorts and t-shirt and work boots, appeared from behind the car. Danny pulled the truck through the gate, and the woman helped me fasten it. "Long drive, huh?" she asked. The wind lifted her hat off her head, and she grabbed it and shoved it back down, smiling all the while.

"Yes, about three hours," I answered. I looked around. An open shed structure with a metal roof was sheltering a large black and white goat who was lying quietly, chewing his cud. "Is that the father?" I asked. She nodded. "How old is he?"

"Two year," she replied. "He two year, girls two year."

Danny was talking to the man. They walked toward us.

"He's pretty good sized for two," Danny said. He was pleased that the father of the goat we wanted to buy was big and attractive. We all walked over to the pen where the other goats were.

"It's a good thing y'all called today," the man said. "We were going to wether him today."

194

Wethering is the practice also called banding, in which a tight band is placed around the skin above the testicles. This cuts off the blood supply, causing the testicles to wither and fall off. It is an easy procedure to keep male animals from reproducing.

"Man, I'm glad we did, too," said Danny. "How old is he?" meaning the buckling.

"Fifteen week," the woman answered, smiling.

"And you want seventy five dollars for him?" asked Danny.

"Yep," said the man, who plopped a camo cotton hat on his head. The chin string settled at the end of his chin, not under it, and the beads at the end of the string swung as he talked.

"Okay," Danny said and went to the truck to get the money.

"So y'all don't live here, just come on the weekends?" I asked.

"Yeah, we come about every other day. Sunday is the only day we have off together, so we come down and spend the night Saturday night in the RV and get up and work on Sundays." They had nice fencing around the perimeter of their property and a holding pen in the middle. A camper was nearby that looked like it was from the same era as the bulldozers.

Danny handed the man the money and asked other questions like how many acres did they have and how long had they owned it, etc, etc.

Soon the man pulled on some too-small leather gloves and said, "Well, let's get him loaded up."

His wife grinned and swung her gray messenger bag around behind her and opened the gate to the holding pen. She strode purposefully over to the little goat, who they had already put an orange rope on, and grabbed the end of the rope with one hand and held onto her floppy hat with the other. The buckling let out a loud bleat when he realized he had been caught and began to struggle. The man picked him up and leaned back to compensate for the weight, and his rotund belly peeked out from under his t-shirt as he carried him to the truck. He set him on the tailgate, but kept holding on to him like he was reluctant to let him go or was afraid he would get away. I lifted the tailgate a little to help trap him, and he pushed the goat on into the truck, and we shut the camper door.

The hat strings were swinging as he peeled off his glove to shake Danny's hand. "Thanks, now. Y'all have a safe trip home." The transaction was finished. I waved to the smiling woman as we drove through the gate, and the goat yodeled his goodbyes from the back of the truck as we drove away, past the antique bulldozers and abandoned old houses, and headed home.

Young Farmhands

Goat farmers are entertaining and personable, and I especially like children who tend the animals. When we went to buy Ariel, Snow White, and Belle, (three guesses who named them) we waited at the gate for the man I had spoken to on the phone. He pulled up as we were petting his Great Pyrenees and scanning the fields for goats. A pretty teenaged girl hopped out to open the gate, and we pulled our truck in behind his. Much to our delight, two more girls, about ten and six, popped out of the truck along with a young man of about twelve who was wearing a straw hat, leather work gloves, and knee high black rubber boots.

The kids told us about their animals. The boy said, "Look down there," pointing down the hill to a field, "See that brown spot? That's a deer. Picasso, like the artist. He stays with that brown cow for protection."

I smiled. "Did you name him? Do you like art?" I asked.

"No, I didn't name him. And yes, I like art," he said.

198

His blue eyes danced as he flashed his pre pubescent, slightly crooked teeth. I was smitten.

His father led us down the hill, and Matthew and his sister Alex, ten, grasped the insulated handles of the electric fence and let us through to the next field. A huge black sow with a chunk missing from her left ear grunted as we approached. Her counterpart, a pale boar, lay on his belly nearby. Tom, the dad, began scratching the hog's back, and he soon turned over to have his underside scratched as well. Two fat miniature donkeys greeted us as we walked through the knee high grass as Carrie, six, tried to mask her excitement at having visitors. Julie, about fourteen or fifteen, swung a leg over one of the donkeys and sat there as Matthew was filling me in on Picasso.

"He'll just come up to you and lick you," he said. The slim deer was wearing a bell that clanked as he made his way toward us. He had a long nose and his legs looked too frail to support his weight, yet he moved gracefully through the pasture toward his master.

The girls giggled as Julie's donkey decided to trot away. Julie just stepped off and laughed as she stumbled and then regained her footing.

Matthew greeted his deer and petted him with his

gloved hands while I took a few pictures and his dad talked with Danny.

A pony, perfectly proportioned except for his midget legs, came trotting up. Alex picked Carrie up and sat her on him. Apparently, he didn't care to be ridden at the moment because he promptly unloaded her onto the hard ground.

Embarrassed and unsure if she was hurt, Carrie began to cry, which surprisingly drew little sympathy from her family.

I, in mama mode, stroked her hair and shoulders and spoke softly to her, asking if she was alright until I noticed no one was paying much attention to her. I suddenly realized I was a stranger who really had no place doing what I was doing.

Her father said, "Carrie, show me the blood. There's no blood; you're okay."

It dawned on me that she was more embarrassed than injured and that she needed something to divert the attention away from her.

"Let's go find those goats," I said to her and we fell in behind the procession that was moving toward the goat herd.

Several of the goats knelt on their front legs.

"Their feet have been wet too long. They're sore. We've got to treat them; it'll get better. Always does," said Tom. We had been getting a fair amount of rain for July, and it was raining lightly as we looked at the animals. We walked on toward the tree line surrounding the field.

"Which ones are girls?" Danny asked. Several baby goats walked around close to their mothers. Tom pointed out three little goats, one white, one black, and one brown.

"I guess that's the ones we want," said Danny. Tom nodded his head, and gestured to the kids.

"Gather them up!" he told them. "Head 'em up toward the house."

The youngsters fanned out behind the goats and herded them along. Carrie, her composure regained, took the lead, gently persuading the goats to climb the hill, something she looked as if she had done before. We followed. The midget pony chased and bit at the big black sow. He was an ornery thing.

As we neared the house, the kids managed to funnel the goats into a gate into a holding pen. When the white doeling passed Matthew, he quickly reached down and grabbed the goat's hind leg, pulled her to him, and picked her up. She bleated loudly and struggled to free herself, but he held on, even with the wild kicking and wiggling. She managed to get him to the ground, and they tumbled over one another as Danny moved to help. Just as he reached them, Snow White got the better of Matthew and escaped. Dang! I thought he had her. She just slipped out of his grasp.

Matt got to his feet and brushed off his jeans as he picked up his straw hat and put it back on. He smiled sheepishly as Danny and I told the plucky young man he made a good try.

"Now, go and get her back in the pen," his dad told him. Matthew shooed the goat through the gate once more.

Danny told me to pull the truck up near the shed where the goats had been herded. Tom and Danny took turns putting the three doelings into the back of the truck and I slammed the camper door shut. It began to sprinkle again as we stood at the back of the truck with Tom and his children. Danny gave Tom the money for the goats and asked him how much he would take for the kids.

"I'd have to pay you to take them," he grinned.

"He wouldn't sell us," Matt said. He said it again

under his breath, looking at the horizon. His eyes flitted from me to Danny. "He wouldn't sell us. He loves us too much," he said, and I wondered if he was trying to convince us or himself.

Danny fished in his wallet. "Well, I want to give the kids something for helping us." He pulled out a few bills while Carrie flashed a wide grin and rocked back and forth on her heels. We only had seven dollars between us after paying for the goats, and I wish I had had more. Tom accepted it on behalf of the children.

"That won't even buy a pizza," I said apologetically.

"I'll put a little with it and it will," said Tom.

I shook hands individually with the smiling children, who were damp and dirty from an afternoon of helping their dad. They were already experienced farmers who loved the humbling duty of taking care of the lives that depended on them. They didn't mind getting dirty and didn't seem to miss the TV and video games. None of them had a cell phone and they didn't step in a cow pile because they were texting. Good job, Tom.

****

We have our own little farmhand in the making. Ellie is learning about life and death on the farm.

One afternoon, she and I were walking in the woods. Ellie stooped down, studying something intently. She dug in the leaves and picked something up. "Whatcha got, El?" I asked her.

"A baby lizard. See?" She thrust a gray two inch creature at me.

"Okay," I said, and she put him in her coat pocket. She had me button the pocket so he couldn't escape, but she kept her hand over the opening for good measure. Still, she couldn't resist taking him in and out.

As we walked back toward the cabin, she pulled him out and studied him intently. I noticed the little guy was quite listless.

I said, "Ellie, I think he's dead."

She held him up by the tail with her left hand and have him a quick poke with her right index finger, which elicited little response, so she shook her left hand a little and he wiggled his legs. Satisfied that he was still with us, she crammed him back in the pocket.

She brought him in the house where Danny was sitting by the stove. When she drew him out to show Papa, but alas, the lizard was dead.

Ellie thought for a moment and said, "I know what

we can do with him."

"You do? What?"

"Feed him to the chickens."

"Well, okay," said Papa.

They went to the chicken pen and she tossed the lizard through the fence and watched as the hens snatched him up.

"I really loved that lizard," she said, and turned to walk in the house.

The One Who Almost Got Away

I decided I wanted to buy a couple of sheep. Sheep are repeatedly used in the Bible as symbols of the children of God, and I wanted to be able to observe them firsthand and see what they are like.

I am partial to black and white animals, and I located a ewe fitting this description in a town near Hot Springs called Benton. We took Ellie and Levi on this sheep buying trip, and everything went fine...for a while.

Since it was getting late in the July afternoon, we decided we would just put the black and white 150 pound ewe and the young white ram in a holding pen at the house in Mountain Valley and take them on up to the cabin the next day. Danny was tired from building cabinets in the heat, so we took the kids home and pulled into the back yard and got out of the truck. I got some rope out of the garage, and Danny made little lassos, opened the camper door, and looped a rope around each of their necks.

Now, you have to understand that sheep are different from goats. When we get new goats, they usually have to be persuaded to get out of the truck. Not sheep. As soon as we lowered the tailgate, they bailed out. Danny had both of the ropes and managed to keep hold of the ram, but the big ewe's rope slid through his hands. I grabbed the ram and threw a leg over his shoulders and held him between my legs. The ewe trotted over to the side of the road and stood there on the hillside baaing at us, the rope dangling from her neck. Danny hurried and put the ram in the pen. We put the dog in the garage to eliminate that source of nuisance and walked slowly toward the ewe. We figured she would come back to the ram because of the herding instinct and because he was calling her. Wrong.

As we approached, she trotted across the street towards our uncle's house. We followed her into his yard, made a few less than graceful attempts to grab her rope as she went by, and watched her helplessly as she ran off into the back of the Walmart parking lot that borders Uncle Junior's property. As I watched her standing on the grassy hillside behind the store, Danny shouted at me to go get the truck and bring it around. "You need to step it up," he said.

I don't do much running these days, but I jogged at a good pace back to our yard and jumped in the truck. By the time I made it to Walmart, Danny was at the gas station next to the highway. The sheep was nowhere to be seen.

"She's done crossed the highway!" Danny said disgustedly as he took the wheel. We took the truck down a gravel lane where he had watched her disappear, and we found her in a little clearing. We got out and chased her around that spot. She was beginning to tire in the heat, and she was panting heavily with a wide open mouth. I didn't know how we would ever get our hands on her.

She disappeared again, this time into the woods with Danny following her. I stood in the grassy clearing sweating and swatting flies and mosquitoes. I decided to just wait until he came back. I started thinking that chiggers were probably about to make a meal of me when I remembered we had some OFF in the truck. I sprayed myself down, and while I waited, I prayed for some help. I was seeing little similarity between the docile Biblical creatures and our new acquisition.

About fifteen minutes later, Danny came out of the woods where he went in, his shirt soaked with sweat and looking pretty exasperated.

"She's over in Philip Partain's field, I think. Let's go over there." We got back in the truck and went down the street and into the big cow pasture.

"Call Connie and let her know what we're doing," he told me. I dialed the number I had looked up on my phone.

"OK," she said, "Just make sure you get the gate shut back."

We drove around the field and saw no sign of the ewe.

"Call Adam and get him to come help us," Danny said. I dialed our son, who lives about five minutes away.

"Can you come help us? We've had a sheep get away from us, and we need help catching her," I said, a little embarrassed.

He laughed. "That's kind of funny," he said. "Ok. Where y'all at?" I told him to meet us in the Partain's field.

We were coming back out of the gate when he arrived.

"I think she must be in that mini storage lot next to this field," Danny told Adam. We drove up to the locked chain link gate and saw a man loading some stuff into his unit. Danny hollered at him and asked him to unlock the gate. He let Danny and Adam in and they drove Adam's Tracker into the lot while I stayed with our pickup outside the gate.

In a few minutes, Danny called me and said, "Come on in, to the very back. She's back here." I had heard the man give Danny the gate code, and I pushed the numbers into the keypad. I drove through the buildings to the back of the lot where the boys were looking at the panting ewe.

I got out, and we made our game plan. There was a shed in one corner of the lot, and we were going to try to force her into the fence corner behind it. The three of us herded her into the corner. Danny was on one end of the shed, Adam on the other with the sheep in between. Danny walked slowly behind her, nudging her toward a crouching Adam, who planned to grab her rope as she came to him. When she got within a few steps, she just jumped over him and ran away.

"Damn," he said. "Wasn't expecting that."

The boys followed her again and trapped her in an area between a row of buildings and a fence. My phone rang in a minute, and Danny said, "Bring the truck around here. We got her."

Yes! I pulled the truck up, and backed it up to where Adam was holding her rope. She was lying on the ground, exhausted. They picked her up, put her in, and slammed the tailgate and camper door.

Man! What a fiasco. I thanked Adam for helping us, and so did his daddy.

The next morning, I texted Adam to offer him lunch:

"Man Subdues Escapee, Saves the Day" A local female eluded captors yesterday, giving chase through the Walmart parking lot, across Hwy 7 N, and through a wooded area before being apprehended in a mini storage lot by Adam Breshears, 29, of Hot Springs. The prisoner managed to break free during a transport to a new facility. Known as "that crazy black bitty" by her warden, the escapee was tackled and brought down at full run by Breshears. She was successfully returned to her captors after being on the lam for about two hours. "I just ran her down," said Breshears, who at one point had been leapt over by the escapee. "She just jumped right over my ass," he said. With level headed strategery, Breshears and his profusely sweating father cornered the offender in a small lane in the mini storage lot where Breshears decided to make his move. "One of us was going down," he said. Much to the relief of bystanders, the convict was apprehended and taken into custody. Breshears is likely to receive a reward of a complimentary meal at the establishment of his choice."

We had pizza the next day, and a couple of weeks passed. To allow the sheep to become accustomed to their new home, we kept the ewe in a holding pen at the cabin. The ram stayed close by, even though he was free to go where he liked. We figured after two weeks had passed, it would be safe to let the ewe out, and she would just fall in with the herd of goats.

Two days after we let her out of the pen, we were driving along the gravel road up to the cabin when we came upon the two wayfarers standing in the road.

"What the crap?" I said. "What are they doing down here?"

Billy Joe and Bobbie Sue, as we had named them after the characters who were on the run in the song 'Take the Money and Run,' looked at us momentarily before stepping into the woods. We devised our plan as we went on up to the cabin to retrieve a feed bucket with grain, a lead rein, and a lariat rope.

We drove back down the mountain and located the sheep, who had thankfully come back onto the road. Danny stopped the Tracker and turned it off. He told me to stay in the car, and he got out and got the feed bucket out and began to shake it. They raised their heads, recognizing the tempting sound that meant supper. He knelt in the road, and they cautiously approached, stretching their necks to get a whiff of the contents of the bucket. He set the bucket down in front of him, and soon they were gobbling up the grain. He made a grab for Bobbie Sue's collar and missed! They trotted back into the woods and stood looking at him suspiciously as he shook the bucket.

Regrouping, Danny looped the lead rein around his body so it wasn't dangling for them to see. He put a little more feed in the can and walked slowly toward the sheep. He sat down, and soon Billy Joe was eating out of the can once more. Danny grabbed his front feet and pinned his head to the ground and wrapped the lead rein around his neck. Ha! Got him. He pulled the ram out into the road and viola! Bobbie Sue followed.

Danny said, "I'll just lead him back up to the cabin. Give us plenty of room before you start the car and come after us."

I watched them disappear around the curve and waited several minutes before I got the Tracker turned around and drove slowly up the road. I crept along, feeling guilty about the trouble I had caused Danny by persuading him to buy sheep when he really didn't want to. He had said they were dumb and thought they would rove. I should have listened.

I was about halfway up the driveway and was looking through the woods to see if I could see them when I heard Danny shout, "Come on up!" I sped up and soon saw them, Danny, breathless and sweating, still holding Billy Joe, and Bobbie Sue standing nearby.

He motioned me to come closer, and as I drew near said, "I'm putting his ass in the car. He hasn't led a step this whole way; I've drug him." He was hot, disgusted, and tired. He opened the back door of the Tracker and flung Billy Joe inside and sat on the tailgate. "Let's go," he said. Bobbie Sue trotted along behind us, baaing the whole way. We put the ram in the holding pen this time, and the ewe stayed near him on the other side of the fence.

I have learned some things during our brief period of sheep ownership. One is I have a good husband who has gone to a lot of trouble for me to indulge my desire to own sheep. I am thankful for his patience. Secondly, in the observations made in relation to the Biblical comparison of God's children to sheep, I can now see how dense and obtuse we can be. Here our Master is providing safety, food and water (spiritual,) companionship, guidance, and love, and we go off on our own, right into the Predator's territory. He tries to show us the way home, but many times we stubbornly refuse to go the way He is showing us, insisting on doing things our own way, following the other sheep instead of the Shepherd. He sometimes puts a rope around our neck and drags us to keep us out of trouble, yet we still struggle because we don't understand that to get back to the barn there is a certain road we have to follow.

God uses many examples from nature to give us a deeper understanding of his word; may we be humble enough to listen.

Back Then

Our house in Mountain Valley is close to Walmart, banks, and other conveniences, but this is not so for the folks in Hollis. Residents now days may go to town every day to work, or retired folks may go to town once a week or so, but in the early days, many families went to town only once or twice a year. Traveling was done on horseback, by wagon, or on foot. Most farms were largely self sufficient, so there was little need to buy things except coffee, sugar, or other things that weren't grown on the farm. The farms in the valley were fertile enough, especially with the delta from the South Fourche River, to grow the crops that are impossible to grow on our rocky hill.

In the typical mountain home, several generations lived together – grandparents, cousins, aunts, and step relatives. The more numerous the family, the more powerful in the community and less dependent they were on others outside their family. These families also depended on each other for entertainment, and often

216

spent evenings after supper playing games, singing, telling stories, giving haircuts, and playing music, all in the yard or on the front porch.

Photos of people from this era with their solemn faces and home haircuts, often wearing threadbare clothing, evoke in me a sense of admiration. Admiration mixed with pity and wonder. I wonder how I would have fared in that time? Would I have been tough enough to chew tobacco as I walked barefoot to school? Could I have had a baby in a sweltering room with no anesthesia? Would I have been content to stay on the farm, or would I have longed for an easier life in the city?

There is a class photo on the wall at the Hawks School that I stood and studied for a while. On the left end, a child dressed in white stands with her hands clasped across her belly. She has short dark hair and is wearing an expression that to me typifies the struggles of the time. She looks like every day is an effort. I wonder if she was hungry the moment the picture was snapped. I wonder if her parents were good to her. I wonder if she was just shy and dubious about school in general and was wallowing in misery, just wanting to be home.

As I sat on one of the benches in the school, I

wondered if I sat in her place. Where did she live? Is she still alive? I don't know, but her image stands out from all the other children in the picture, and I wish I could talk to her, but she is held prisoner behind the glass.

There were few doctors around in the pioneer days. The child in the picture, like most babies, was probably born with a midwife or neighbor in attendance. Brothers and sisters were often sent to neighbors for the birth of a new baby and then were summoned home to welcome the infant. Married women's task in life (among others) was to have babies. "Barefoot and pregnant" was not derogatory; it was pretty accurate, and the women accepted it and gloried in it. Having numerous healthy babies was something to be proud of. The best way to hire laborers was to produce them; that's the way it was and no one stood around on crates in the town square screaming that it wasn't fair.

In those days it was customary to stay in bed nine days after the birth of a child and to stay at home for thirty. Older girls and single female relatives helped the new mother with her chores and with the baby, something new moms now rarely get to enjoy, at least for that lengthy period of time. Dads didn't help with housework. It simply wasn't his place to do women's work any more than it was expected of a woman to do men's work.

Many mothers used an old dry goods box with rockers added for a crib for the newborn. She could rock with her foot as she mended the family's sparse wardrobe. Women have always had an ability to multitask. I have washed dishes with one hand and held the baby on my hip while talking on the phone as the spaghetti begins to boil and the washer and dryer toil in the background.

Many new parents vow they will not give their baby a pacifier, a notion that is usually abandoned the first fussy night. An early version of the pacifier was called a sugar tit- a mixture of crumbled biscuits sprinkled with sugar and butter, dissolved with hot water, poured into a porous cloth and given to a cranky infant to suck on. The first time I heard the term was from my father-in-law making a comment about a frail looking young man, "He looks like he ought to still be home sucking a sugar tit."

Before little glass jars of Gerber Baby Food, what was a mother to do? Well, she would chew the food in her own mouth then give it to the baby. You gotta do what you gotta do.

Babies wore long dresses, both boys and girls. The

baby's dress touched the floor when the mom stood up, and wasn't cut off til baby started crawling. The cutting of the dress was a milestone in baby development, an event bragged about like a first tooth. Boys wore dresses until about age four. Boy dresses buttoned down one side, girls down the front, so the sex of the child could be known, much like pink and blue are used as signals today.

Unfortunately, the infant mortality rate was high. A baby who didn't survive was buried in a homemade coffin, covered in white sateen, inside and out. Two neighbor women may hold coffin in their laps in a wagon to go to the graveyard.

What a sad and solemn event. The death of a child is probably the most heart wrenching and scarring thing a parent can go through. The local cemeteries with their tiny headstones are a sad reminder of the precious lives lost. Just because losing a baby was common doesn't mean it was easy.

Kids grew up tough. They had to to survive. They learned skills and were depended upon to pull their share of the load around the house. Six- year- olds fed chickens, gathered eggs, ground coffee, and gathered firewood. In a couple of years, they would be expected to work in the fields alongside the adults. Girls cooked family meals, milked cows, churned butter, did sewing and mending – everyone had to contribute to make the farm successful. No iPhones or Xboxes or obesity. Kids took on adult habits fairly early, and not just work habits. Children as young as six chewed tobacco or dipped snuff as a treatment for dyspepsia.

When the youngsters marked the sixth or seventh birthday, most started school if one was nearby. Location of streams often dictated which school a child would attend. Children might walk an extra mile or two to attend one on his side of the creek to avoid having to cross when it was flooded or cold, a fact stated to me first hand by a couple of interviewees. School houses had two doors, the left usually the one for boys, the right one for girls. Sexes were kept strictly separated. When the boys lined up in front of the left door, they filed into the school room and took their places on the left side of the room, and the girls did the same on the right side. Separate buckets for drinking water were also kept. If there was only one bucket, there were separate dippers. At recess games were segregated as well.

At lunch time the students would pull out their pails

and see what their mother had sent. Biscuits made with white flour were common fare, along with fried potatoes with salt meat, baked sweet potatoes, typically carried in an eight pound lard tin. All the children from one family ate from the same pail. Cheaper cornbread was eaten by the kids whose mothers couldn't buy white flour. A mother might include jars of butter and molasses for biscuits. Lunch was finished with fried peach or apple pies. Jars of milk or buttermilk kept cool in the stream until lunchtime was sometimes brought as a treat and to have something different to drink than water.

In the early days of the Ouachita frontier, adventuresome boys who weren't busy with chores or school would bait a snare with salt and catch a free ranging horse, ride it bareback, and turn it loose. An early form of joyriding, I suppose.

Custom dictated fashion to a large degree. Knee britches, like those mentioned by Perk Dickson, were worn until boys were considered old enough to go with the girls. A girl could not date someone who still wore knee britches, so some controlling fathers kept their sons in knee britches long after he was past the age to move into the more manly long pants.

Courting couples were often involved in a lengthy courtship due to the fact that their families were reluctant to give up the help that would leave when they married. A young woman and young man were naturally very productive and strong, and their families needed them. However, when the two became able to get some land and some sort of dwelling, they moved out and the cycle of raising children and farming the land was begun again. 8

I can't help but compare the people of those pioneer generations to ours. I am not naïve enough to think everyone was industrious and honest and hardworking because they aren't all that way now. There is nothing new under the sun and man has a basic nature, but it seems that slackeredliness wasn't tolerated then like it is now. Well, back then if you didn't do the work, you went hungry and naked, not something most folks enjoyed. It would do my heart good to see some of these young men pull up their dang pants and pitch some hay.

Edith Cox Owens

It was hot. The midsummer grass had lost its color and looked tired, like a man coming in from working on Saturday. The white house with the green metal roof sat on a knoll, its yard defined by a chain link fence with an open gate. A wooden chair was tied to a pine tree about six feet off the ground, and in its seat was a cobweb covered bird feeder that hadn't had guests in a while. Three well fed dogs greeted me as I opened my car door to visit with Edith Cox Owens.

The porch was closed in with storm windows, and I knocked on the accompanying glass door. When I got no response, I rapped louder with my remote on my keyring. The front door creaked open, and Mrs. Owens appeared. She unlocked the storm door and invited me in. A large window unit air conditioner was humming loudly from its perch in a window next to the front door, and its condensation was being collected in buckets to keep from ruining the porch floor. As we went in, one of the more assertive dogs took advantage of the open door and scurried past us, wagging his tail. "He knows I'll give him a treat to get him to go out the back door," she said as she went to get the bait.

I took a seat on the couch while Mrs. Owens, in her red and white striped shirt and cornflower blue colored pants cut off just above her knees, escorted her dog out. She came back to the living room and took a place in a floral recliner whose twin was close by. She looked at me through her bifocal glasses and patted her brown hair.

"I was born right here in this room," she said. "Right over there." She pointed to a corner of the room where a wide screened TV sat next to an antique radio. Above the radio hung a large sepia portrait of a man and woman, her great grandparents. "That painting behind you is of this house. You can see that there are a lot more trees around it now; my grandmother had my grandad keep the pines cut, but I like them and have let them grow."

She told me how her family came to own her land. "My great grandmother homesteaded this place. Her first husband, Sam Johnson, went to the Confederate Army and he never did come home. Never knew what happened to him. So she married my great grandfather; he had been in the same war. He was carrying the mail from Dardanelle on a horse. He'd come around, and he met her down here at her place on South Fourche. He homesteaded some more land, and then my grandfather inherited the land from them." Mrs. Owens's family has managed to maintain ownership of over three hundred acres.

Edith had her own book project, a compilation of family histories and genealogical information of the Steve, Onyx and Graham communities. She and cousin Alpha Jane Hull Gossett wrote *Echoes of the Valley, a history of the South Fourche Valley of Central Arkansas* in 1998. The ladies contacted members of the community and their descendents to gather information to record for posterity. Sadly, Mrs. Gossett died before the book was completed, but Mrs. Owens, wanting to see the project through, typed the collected information on an electric typewriter late at night after her aging mother had gone to bed. A copy of the book lay on the coffee table in front of me, and I asked to look at it, and to buy a copy. I purchased one of her last two copies.

As we discussed the book, Snowball, a white cat with brown spots, jumped to the arm of her owner's chair, sat down, and placidly began to lick herself. Mrs. Owens said, "My granddaughter had never heard the word 'snowball' before I named this cat so she called her Eyeball."

Edith lived in the white house with the green roof until she was thirteen. Then she went to Plainview to live with a young woman whose husband was in the Army and was expecting a baby. She wanted someone to stay with her, so Edith boarded with her while she went to high school at Plainview.

"What was it like, living with someone like that? Did you know her well?" I asked.

"Not really. I knew *of* her. It was strange." For a thirteen year old girl going from living on a remote farm to living in town with a casual acquaintance must have been an adjustment.

"My aunt knew her better than I did. I helped her with the dishes. She wanted someone to get up and build a fire in the mornings because she was pregnant. I didn't do much housework. The house was just a two bedroom, with a living room and kitchen, in Plainview, not on a farm or anything. I only stayed with her about one year. She had her baby about the middle of the time that I stayed there. I was not too much into babies at that time. I held him or changed him when he needed it, but I didn't do a whole lot to his upkeep," she chuckled. I'm sure the young teenager had other things on her mind than minding a baby. She went home on weekends.

The next year Mrs. Owens stayed with her aunt and cousins during the school year which was more like home. She said she and her cousins "strolled the streets" because there was nothing else to do. They didn't have a car.

"There was a movie house and it changed movies three times a week, so once you went and saw it, you were out until it changed again."

She recalled a time when she was a child in the first grade. The Steve school was about a mile from her home. "I didn't like school. I remember one day telling the teacher I was sick, so he had my brother bring me home. Bless my little old brother's heart, he carried me on his back. There wasn't anything wrong with me, I just wanted to come home. Mother never did find that out, that I wasn't feeling bad, because she would not have liked that."

She had fond memories of her teachers at the one room schoolhouse. "They were all very nice people; they did not whip you a lot. I had an uncle named Pearl Hull, and he was a special man. I remember this boy, this kid, one day, he just would not mind Uncle Pearl. It just didn't matter what Uncle Pearl told him; he just didn't mind him.

Now this was back when a nickel was a nickel. Uncle Pearl pulled a nickel out of his pocket, and he said, 'If you'll behave, I'll give you this nickel,' and the kid behaved. Instead of whipping him, Uncle Pearl used that theory on him, and he behaved."

I asked her what it was like in that one room school as a first grader. She looked at the gas space heater on the wall. "You just sat in your seat until recess. When it got your time to learn anything, they called you up to the front, and you went up there, and they had you read, or had you spell, or do arithmetic. That's about the only three subjects we had."

The telephone rang, and she excused herself to answer the cordless phone that sat on the table alongside and old push button phone. As she talked about meeting someone at the Nooner Cemetery to choose a grave site, I looked around the room. A quilt rack hung from the ceiling and a corner cabinet housed a collection of pink depression glass. There was a gray towel hanging from a rod over the glass in the front door. Snowball jumped to the floor and chased an itch on his backside then walked into the kitchen where rows of cookie jars lined the tops of the cabinets.

When Mrs. Owens hung up, I asked her about the third phone in the room, the wooden one on the wall.

"That was used here. In fact, up here, my grandmother had two mounted up there on the wall. And from down the road, if they wanted to talk to anybody past here, they called her. She had a switch, and she would ring these people up here, and she would put that switch down and they could hear each other. She was kind of like Telephone Central."

This phone operator grandmother, Nannie Jones Sims, taught Edith how to quilt, crochet and embroider.

"What was she like?" I asked.

"My grandmother? What would I say about her? My grandmother loved to clean house. She loved new things, she loved learning to do new things, she set a table that you would go into the kitchen and think, 'Well, she hasn't got anything to fix,' and when she got through, the table was full of food. She was a very, very, special person. You didn't sit idle. No. She taught me to crochet and embroidery and all the skills they did back then. She'd just sit you down and say, 'This is the way you do it,' and you didn't do it sloppy; she'd make you take it out."

She described her grandparents' relationship.

"I don't know that either one was the boss, to tell you the truth. I don't ever remember them arguing about anything. He had his job, and she had her job, and they did it and didn't fuss about it. My grandpa was a quieter person. He was not as industrious as my grandmother." She smiled. "He might have planted fifty pounds of potatoes where she'd plant a hundred."

She related how the families in the communities coexisted. "They had a really good relationship. There was not any fighting; there was just good companionship. And still today, there's very few of us left, but the few that are still living, I just think of us as one big family. I think there's some of the best people in the world that lives up and down this valley."

Perk Dickson's Funeral

The notes of "Go Rest High on the Mountain" drifted into the fellowship hall where the overflow crowd was seated. "Son, your work on earth is done." People were standing and seated in the back room of the Pentecostal church facing the wall that separated the auditorium from the fellowship hall. We sat quietly trying our best to hear the preacher as he talked about Perk Dickson. The main auditorium of the church was full of Perk's immediate family. I and his numerous friends had squeezed into the aisles and sat in the black chairs in the fellowship hall where food for the family was waiting on tables along the far wall. The smell of beans wafted through the air as the crowd, dressed in everything from suits and dresses to jeans and plaid shirts to camouflage, came to pay their respects to the man who had obviously been well loved by his community.

The preacher, whose voice became quivery at times, spoke of Perk saving a man named Tom Crawford who had cut himself with a chainsaw. "Perk put that man on his shoulder and carried him out. You know, he'll get a crown for that." I thought to myself, 'That's not all he'll get a crown for.' The one time I got to visit with Mr. Dickson, he was so entertaining and engaging that I suspected he was a popular guy. Now as I sat among the crowd of about three hundred people, my suspicions were confirmed.

After several songs about heaven and peace, a slide show started that featured Perk and his family. My view was obscured by two aging deputies who were on duty to work the funeral. They had come inside to escape the July heat. I could only see the edges of the screen around their hats. I could only see glimpses of Perk's life.

When the preacher finally closed, the crowd began to file past the black casket with the silver colored handles. Perk lay in quiet repose in a brand new pair of overalls and beautiful plaid shirt. His widow, who he had married forty seven years ago after her first husband had died in the well, sat teary eyed in a wheelchair in the front row and watched in the bewilderment that accompanies fresh widowhood as the well wishers paid their last respects.

The funeral was over. I stepped out into the bright sunshine. The air was hot and steamy with Arkansas summertime humidity, and I thanked the Lord for letting me meet Mr. Perk Dickson and for the things he accomplished in a life that was lived in a small place, but in a big way.

Conclusion

During the months I worked on the manuscript for this book, the people I had met swam through my mind along with my early nursing years when I worked the night shift. They showed up in my dreams.

I had come to the hospital to relieve a sick co worker in the middle of the shift. No one had time to give me report on my patients so I just made rounds to make sure everyone was doing all right. As my white shoes floated down the shiny floor, my breath fogged as if I were in a freezer. Silently I pushed open the door to room 304.

In the bed a tanned young man with hard muscles lies sleeping with his mouth hanging open. He has no teeth because the chainsaw that kicked back and cut his face knocked them out. The bandages on his face and neck need to be changed; his blood is soaking through the gauze, whispering to me what happened in the woods. He is in the merciful stupor of morphine right now and watches his friend helping him in the truck like he is watching a movie. I, in my dream state, am in the theater, too.

Now I am looking in on the patient in Room 305. An elderly man, at least ninety, is awake and says, "Hon, will you empty this urinal? I can't use it 'cause it's so full." He is sitting up in bed, wearing a jacket with a torn sleeve. He is smoking a cigarette and flipping ashes into a dark green ashtray that sits next to a can of Coke.

As I pour the urine into the toilet, I am wondering how he got permission to smoke in the hospital. I flash to his house and he is showing me an Indian game ball. Then I am back at his bedside. He has a broken hip and has a foam boot around his foot and ankle with a five pound weight attached to a rope that is affixed to the boot hanging off the bed. Buck's traction. Prevents muscle spasms. Must remember to chart that. He tells me he will have surgery tomorrow and asks me if I want to drive out to Marble Hill and see that grave.

306. The door to her room is made of screen, and it bangs shut behind me. The patient is behind a cash register wearing a hospital gown as she talks to her customers. Three young men in plaid shirts with long beards are paying for some Bugler tobacco in a blue can, then they ask her if they can sell some baskets outside her room in the hall. I ask her if she knows anyone I can interview, but she

only wants to talk about the tests she is having tomorrow.

When I go into Room 307, a frail looking man wearing oxygen is sitting in a wheelchair next to his hospital bed. He is wheezing and coughing. Got to call Respiratory. "Sit down right here." He points to a chair next to his bed, and he is telling me of drowning boys and dead men in a well and dancing. I turn on my recorder and look out his plate glass window and see my car in his driveway.

"How's my buddy across the hall doin'?" he asks. "I thought I'd never get him in here. That train at Jessieville held us up. Did that doctor get his teeth put back in?"

In room 308, a woman with a 1930's hairdo is sitting on the edge of her bed writing by the light of a coal oil lamp. Her sun browned arm and hand have nice plump veins and I think starting an IV would be easy. She smiles when she sees me. "I'm writing a book," she says. "I'm only here for the night. I pulled something in my back when I was moving furniture out of the living room for the square dance." A man is lying on a cot with his face to the wall, sleeping. She ignores him.

I tell her I'm writing a book, too. When I tell her I think we may be neighbors, she is delighted. She says she has some extra flower bulbs that she dug up at an old home place near hers and asks me if I want some- invites me to come by her place on Rocky Crossing - a neighborly thing to do.

Again I am in the hallway, but now it is completely dark. I hear a bird softly singing, chirping a soothing melody. It is the middle of the night. Birds should be in bed with the lights off so they don't bother their roommates. Still, the singing persists. I cock my head to listen a little, to hear the gentle notes calling me, guiding me out of my dreamy confusion. Calling me back to reality, back to my mountain top cabin, back to my goats and my love, calling me back to Hollis.

The End

Addendum

While I was writing *Living at Hollis,* I spent a good deal of time wondering about Charlie May Simon. It was upon my learning that Ms. Simon had lived in the community that I was inspired to research the history of Hollis and interview its residents. I traveled to Little Rock to the library at the Arkansas Studies Institute, which housed several boxes of Ms. Simon's photos, early manuscripts, scrap books with numerous newspaper articles of her book releases, and printed book reviews. I was excited to find a photo of the cabin she and Howard Simon built on Rocky Crossing. There were photos of her and Howard and later pictures of her and third husband, Pulitzer Prize winning poet, John Gould Fletcher. As I poured over the silent images, I realized there were many details I would never know.

I let my imagination fill in the gaps and wrote a fictional account of Charlie May's days at Hollis.

Going for Broke

Paris, France 1929

Charlie May Simon glided into the ballroom with her fur trimmed green coat clinging to her slight frame. Her tam fit closely over her eton crop hairdo, and her earrings dangled against her white neck. She spotted her husband, Howard, smoking, talking and laughing with a group of men with lacquered hair, all of them dressed in black tuxedos and shiny shoes. She raised a gloved hand to him, and he waved her over, cigarette in one hand, and an ice clinking drink in the other.

"Ah, Charlie May! At last. I want you to meet Fletcher here. John Gould Fletcher," he boomed as he took his wife's arm. "This is my pride and joy, Charlie May Simon."

"Charmed," said Fletcher as he kissed her hand.

"The Nobel prize winner in poetry? That John Gould Fletcher?" asked Charlie May.

He smiled his confirmation as he released her hand, but held her gaze. "I understand we have something in common."

Charlie May raised her eyebrows. "Oh?"

"Arkansas. I was born in Little Rock."

"Oh really? I'm from Monticello."

"I know. I've read your work."

She smiled and dropped her eyes.

"John," Howard said, "Be a chum and entertain my lovely wife for a while, won't you? I hear the billiard room calling. You two go ahead and have a chat about Arkansaaaw," He laughed at himself and kissed his wife lightly on the cheek then turned to go.

"Don't be too long, dear, I'm famished."

"Righto," he said. "See you in a bit."

Hollis, Arkansas, 1930

Two men sat outside on the bench, one with tobacco spit stains streaking his gray beard and the other with a too-big hat that pushed his ears down so they stuck out like two upside down bookends. Howard swung open the screen door for Charlie May and it sprang shut behind them. The wooden floor was uneven and the air smelled of coffee and woodsmoke, even though there was no fire in the stove. Dennis and Lilly Crain were behind the counter, and Lilly was putting birdseed into Delph's little box in her cage.

"How you folks doin?" asked Dennis.

"Fine," said Charlie May. "How's Delph?" She put her finger to the edge of the cage and clucked as the mynah bird turned her head sideways to inspect her customers.

"Finern frog's hair," said Lilly as she closed the cage. "Whach youns need today?"

"Just some coffee and a newspaper. Is the Little Rock paper here?" Charlie May asked.

"Yesm. Right ovair by the tabaccy," she said, pointing at the stack of papers on the shelf next to the Bull Durham tobacco and square brown bottles of Garrett snuff. Charlie May picked up a paper and scanned the headlines. **No Relief in Sight - Empire State Building Opens - New National Anthem.**

"Say, Mizz Simon," Lilly said with a toothless grin. "You want to see my new piglets? They's right cute."

Charlie May smiled. "Yes!" she said, "I'd love to," and followed her out the back door.

Dennis asked Howard, "How's the cabin comin?"

"Sumbitch." Delph said quietly.

Dennis laughed and shrugged his shoulders. "I don't know wheer she learnt to talk like that."

Howard smiled. "The cabin is okay. A little leaky."

"Yeah, we been a havin the rain, ain't we? Thatn last night was a toad strangler. Oh, yeah," he said, reaching into one of the little square boxes behind him, "Your wife got a letter."

"Thanks." He slipped it in his pocket. "I guess I need some cigarettes, too."

"Asshole," said Delph.

"Which uns do you use? Lucky Strikes?"

"No, Camels."

He laid a pack on the counter. "Say, Simon, about your bill..."

Howard bristled.

"I'm a gonna hafta cut youns off. I cain't afford to...."

"Right. I'll get you some money as soon as I can."

"I cain't let youns have no more after today."

Charlie May and Lilly were laughing as they came in the back door. "Howard, you ought to see Lilly's baby pigs. They're so cute! They're in heaven in this mud."

"I know where you're going with that, dear. No

pigs."

"You're no fun," said Charlie May. She turned to Lilly. "We'll talk later," she said and winked.

Delph whistled and said, "Look at that chassis! Hide the hooch. Hide the hooch." She ruffled her feathers and eyed the birdseed and gave it a quick peck.

Dennis reddened a little. "I'm sorry, ma'am. We don't know wheer that bird's been. We ain't got no hooch around here."

"She's charming," said Charlie May. "Reminds me of some people I know."

"Well, let's go," said Howard. "See if this old flivver will start up."

"Asshole," said Delph.

The Studebaker had seen better days. After several cranks, it fired up, lurched onto the road, and slid into the muddy ruts. Howard didn't even need to steer, just accelerate and brake. The car grunted and complained all the way up the mountain, and he cursed it as if he were aboard a stubborn mule. The tires slung mud onto the running boards and occasionally sent a blob into Charlie May's lap or face, which she brushed away without comment.

"When you were outside, Dennis Crain said that today was the last time he was going to let us charge anything," said Howard.

"Really? Well, you can hardly blame him. Everybody in the valley has a bill at the store."

The car coughed and heaved as they turned down Rocky Crossing Road. Howard said, "I hope we make it home. I really don't want to hoof it in this mud."

"Well, a little dirt never hurt anybody. What was that Orwell said? 'To survive it is often necessary to fight, and to fight you have to dirty yourself.' "

Howard tightened his grip on the wheel and worked his jaw muscles. The mud was pissing him off and so was his wife.

"We sure have gotten dirty since we've been here." He shook his head. How could she stay so optimistic? To him, Arkansas was hell.

"You know, I'm getting a little sick of your Pollyanna attitude." Living in Arkansas was not what he had expected.

"What?"

"Yeah. You and your 'Let's go to Arkansas and homestead. We can live off the land,'" he said in a mocking

245

tone. "'It won't cost us a thing. No money,' she says." He rolled his eyes. "Marymotheragod. I don't care if your grandfather did homestead in this 'neck of the woods,' This was a piss poor idea to move to this podunk, backwoods, prehistoric place. What the hell was I thinking, letting you talk me into this?"

"You were thinking we wanted to live, Howard. You weren't selling art; I wasn't selling books, people couldn't afford luxuries anymore. They were like us - broke."

"And we're better off here? We're still broke, in case you haven't noticed."

Charlie May shrugged. She watched the trees drop big splats of water to the forest floor as they drove along. She thought about their creditors in New York, how they had left without notice. "I still feel bad for moving off and leaving our debts. We were about to go under, though."

"Go under? We were drowning like bastard puppies in a bag full of rocks. I don't know why you feel bad. Nobody could pay their bills. I don't feel bad about leaving New York City in debt. I feel bad about ruining my Studebaker on these pigtrails," said Howard. "Just look at her."

The filthy car lurched into the yard of the sagging

little log cabin sitting on a knoll backdropped by the mountains. Howard killed the engine, and they got out and slogged over to the garden patch that was surrounded by a fence made from cedar saplings strung together with rusty wire. It leaned here and there like it was tired and needed to rest. They watched the skinny chickens milling about searching for a crumb or a bug - anything they might have missed. The greedy little rooster found a grandaddy long legs and gobbled it up before the others could notice, then strutted about, proud of his secret victory. The scattered corn and purple hull pea plants were beaten down and lay in quiet resignation on the mud.

"This is pathetic. This whole place is pathetic," said Howard. "I...."

Charlie May cocked her head and listened. She put her finger to her lips to shush Howard's grousing. "Someone's coming."

Several young men were walking down Rocky Crossing Road. Their heads appeared over the hilltop, followed by the rest of their bodies. The mud blended their pants and bare feet into one, turning them into statues from the ground up. One young man caught sight of the Simons and waved. "Hey!"

Howard and Charlie May smiled and waved back. The boys squished into the yard.

"Youns got any water handy?"

"Sure," said Howard. "Lots of it."

The boys laughed. "We's needin a drank," said one of them.

"Oh, sure. Let's draw some." Howard stepped over to the spring fed well and let down the bucket and pulled it back out. "Where are you boys headed?"

"Oh, down at the river. We's gonna set out some trout lines. Them catfish ourght to be a bitin in this high water." He turned to a companion. "Getcha a drank Gerald," he said, handing him the dipper, "This is that good ole sprang water."

"Aren't you Perk Dickson?" Howard asked the boy.

"Yessir."

"I thought I recognized you. I've seen you at the store."

"Yessir, I knowed who you was. My daddy and Uncle Harley come up here and hept with your house raisin. I woulda come, save I was sick with a fever."

"Oh, that's all right. We really appreciated all the help."

Perk spat on the ground and studied the pitiful garden. "Looks like your garden got drownded. Didja plant by the light a the moon?"

"No. You mean at night?"

"Naw." The other boys snickered. Charlie May smiled. "Between the new moon and the full moon. You gotcherself about eight days a good plantin time for thangs that grow above the ground like peas and okry. You wanna plant by the dark a the moon for your taters and beets and sech." The rest of the young men nodded knowingly. "Hit takes a whaal to git it down. Purty soon you'll have er."

They picked up their gear and walked to the road, hopping on the higher patches of ground that stood out of the water. "Thanks for the drank." Perk yelled over his shoulder.

Charlie May waved from the porch. She slid off her boots, rolled up her pants, and went inside. Warmer days were coming, but the evenings were chilly and the nights were cold. Howard still hadn't chopped any wood. She hung her cap on the peg on the back of the door and absently tried to fluff her flattened hair as she walked into the kitchen. Her husband's easel was next to the window that framed the distant Ouachita icon, Forked Mountain.

She looked at the mountain at the sun casting long rays across its twin peaks. One peak was lower than the other in an ancient deference – the lesser one looking straight ahead, more level on top, and the taller peak more jagged and unsettled, always yearning to touch the sky. A half finished painting of the scene had been sitting on the easel for weeks with little pots of dried up acrylics on the table nearby.

Charlie May's typewriter was in the bedroom. Howard didn't like to hear the clacking when he painted, but she didn't mind closing the door between them. She worked better alone.

Howard stood looking at the muddy garden glanced over his shoulder at the lopsided cabin. House raising indeed. Some comparison to his sixteenth floor apartment in New York City. *I wish I'd never come here.* What this mud needed was a little concrete. *'Hit just takes a whaal.'* Yeah, I'd like to see how long you lasted in my neighborhood. <u>You'd</u> get planted by the light of the moon.* The Studebaker, once gleaming and sleek, now looked more like a wagon than a car. Charlie May had insisted on putting a wooden bed over the trunk to haul supplies in. *What a hokey piece of shit. I'll never get out of here.*

Howard snorted and shoved his hands in his pockets. *What's this?* He felt the envelope the postmaster had given him at the store. He snatched it out and looked at the address. Charlie May Simon, Hollis, Arkansas. The return address read John Gould Fletcher, New York City. *What the hell?* He slid his finger under the flap and tore it open.

Dear Charlie May,

I've been thinking about when I met you in Paris. When I looked into your eyes and kissed your hand, there was an embryonic joining of our souls. Born of that union are ever present images that have seeped into the deepest vortexes of my mind, and now they lie there mesmerizing me, unashamedly seducing me, until I can think of little else. I am a parched nomad searching for the oasis of your touch and a man overboard drowning in a river of desire.

Are you well in the state of our birth? Does the homeland womb that propelled us both forth now sustain and protect you? I dream of you in the mountains where I'm told you now live and picture your ivory cheeks flushed pink by the wild breezes and your skin golden from the sun's sweet caress. How I burn with envy of that fortunate sun - that sun who is able to touch you while I cannot.

Oh, to grasp the apparition who visits my chambers and haunts every moment! To have you materialize and touch your quivering lips-to hear your whispers and groanings soft and warm on my ear- to feel your smooth skin on mine, to taste the ambrosia of your mouth...

Curse Venus and Aphrodite with their myrtle crowns! I am Pothos in chains! Dip your finger in the water and cool my blazing. Come to me ~ John

Howard's ears burned with anger. *Damn big timer moving in on my wife. If he was here right now......*He kicked at the fence post. *First those sappy inbreeds making fun of me while she grinned -thought it was cute-that bastard at the store-and now this! I'm married to a cuddler, a real quiff. What did they do at that party? I'll fix that bitch. I'm gonna beat it. By myself.*

He stomped up the steps and into the cabin.

"Hey," Charlie May said. "Take off those shoes."

"Take off my shoes? Don't you boss me, woman."

"I'm not..."

"I'll dance on the table in these shoes if I want to. I'll roll around on the bed and rub chicken shit all over it if

252

I want to!"

"What?"

"Oh, please. I'm tired of your country woman charade, Miss Homesteader. You acted like you knew what those gumps were talking about in the yard. You thought it was funny that they made me look like a fool, like some Palooka."

"No, I didn't.....Howard...I...."

"And at the store...." He thought of the letter in his pocket and reached to get it, then thought better of it. He would never give her the satisfaction. "Dennis Crain is shutting us off, and you're on *his* side. I'm fed up with all this, this ... Here," he said. "I'll show you what I think of your garden, your chickens, your leaky cabin, and your whole Arkansas mountain homesteading shit." He unzipped his pants and peed on the floor at her feet, splashing urine on her stockings.

She stood and reached for the shotgun hanging over the fireplace. "Get the hell out of here, Howard, before I paper the wall with your guts."

"Oh, don't worry. I'm going. I'm writing the goddam Declaration of Independence. I don't care if you rot in these woods!" He grabbed his dried up paints and brushes and threw them into a box and stormed into the bedroom and grabbed a couple of pairs of pants and shirts and crammed them in with his supplies.

"I'm leaving, and I'm taking the car. What's left of it." He left a trail of muddy footprints across the small living room, and Charlie May watched him descend the steps and throw the box into the Studebaker. He gunned the engine and let out the clutch, spinning the tires and slinging mud into the garden and on the front of the house. The car fishtailed out into the road and disappeared.

She sat down in a wobbly chair at the table, stunned. *Where did that come from?* She shook her head in disbelief. *I knew he missed New York, but...really...gumps in the yard? I didn't laugh at him. Country woman charade? Good Lord.* She laid the gun across the table and rested her head on her folded arms. *What a baby! What am I going to do out here by myself?* She raised her head, suddenly aware of how alone she was. There weren't even locks on the doors. No dog to bark. The chickens were the only other living beings on the place. *Maybe I'll talk to Lilly about a couple of those pigs. And a dog.* She looked at the typewriter sitting in the bedroom on a table next to the bed. The *Robin on the Mountain* manuscript was nearly finished. *I've got to wrap that up and send it to Dutton. Oh, Lord. This gun isn't even loaded. Ha! Howard didn't know that. Paper the wall with your guts! As if he had any. Do I have any shells?* She got up and lifted the lid on the round wooden cheese box on the mantle and tiptoed to look inside. There were six buck shots. She picked up two, broke the gun, inserted one in each barrel, and snapped it shut. She replaced it on the pegs over the fireplace and wiped her sweaty palms on her pants. *That's better. Son of a bitch better not come back.*

Excited voices rang through the trees. *That must be those boys.* She looked out the window. They were trotting and hopping down the road as quickly as they could. One boy had his arms slung over the shoulders of two of his friends. He was soaking wet and could barely walk. They hurried into her yard.

"What's the matter?" she called as she hurried down the steps.

"Gerald pert near drowned. He was leanin' out over the river tyin a trout line, and he fell in. Perk jumped in after 'eem and pulled 'eem out. He's plum give out."

"Bring him up here on the porch."

They laid the listless boy on the plank floor and

255

stood back with their hands on their hips and waited, like she could magically make him all right. His teeth were chattering and his eyes rolled back in his head. "Get some quilts off the bed." Charlie May shouted. "We've got to get these wet clothes off of him." She unbuckled his overalls, and the boys slid them off. He was wearing no underwear.

"Gimme that blanket," one of them said and threw it over Gerald. "Sorry, ma'am."

"Where's Perk?" she asked, looking around.

"Yonder he comes." Perk was trudging up the road, soaking wet.

"How's he a doin'?" he yelled as he came in the yard. He climbed the steps and looked at Gerald. "Reckon he's gonna be all right?" He coughed and rubbed his face.

"I don't know. Get some dry clothes for Perk," Charlie May said. One of the boys went into the house. He came back with a pair of Charlie May's pants and one of Howard's shirts. She started to say something, but thought her pants would fit him better anyway. The boy thrust the clothes at Perk, who was shivering in the late afternoon dampness. "Kin I change in the shed?"

"There is no shed. Go in the house."

"Yes'm."

Gerald was beginning to quiet. "You fellas go on down and get his mother and father. Have them bring a car."

"They ain't got no car, ma'am."

"See if they can borrow one." The boys hurried through the yard and down the road chattering nervously. Perk appeared in the doorway, his pants four inches too short and his sleeves covering his hands.

"Should I build a far?" he asked.

"Yes, we need to get Gerald warmed up."

Perk went to the wood pile and picked up the splitting maul and set a log on its end. He swung it and easily split the log in two. Soon he had a pile of firewood. "You got any kindlin'?"

"No, I don't think so."

"Let me see iffn I find some pine," he said as he looked toward the woods.

"Gerald, do you think you can get up and come in the house?"

He opened his eyes and looked at her but then closed them again. She looked at the clock on the mantle through the open door. 5:30. It would probably be dark by the time his parents got here. Charlie May went to the

257

bucket of water Howard had drawn for the boys. *Was that really only an hour ago?* She got a dipperful for Gerald. She raised his head and put it to his lips. He took a small drink and laid his head back down. *Where is Perk?*

The boy stepped out of the woods with an armful of rich pine. He went in the house and quickly built a fire.

"Let's get Gerald in there," Charlie May said, and they each took an arm and pulled him into the cabin and laid him near the stove.

"This ourghta getcha warmed up there, feller."

Charlie May watched Perk's face as he looked worriedly at Gerald. "The boys said you saved him."

He blushed a little. "I's just doin' my duty."

"Mmm."

Perk stared into the flames. "He was goin' under. I had to hep eem. Weren't no choice."

She followed the spot where his eyes were transfixed and stared with him.

"Sometimes we don't have choices, do we, Perk?"

"Nome."

"Were you scared?"

"Yes'm, I reckon I was."

They sat in silence while Gerald slept. It was growing

dark when they heard the sputter of the Model T coming up the road.

"Would you like to do some chores for me sometime? I don't have any money, but I'd cook for you."

"Yes'm. I reckon I would."

Gerald's whole family piled out of the car and rushed to the cabin. "Oh, Lordy!" his mother shouted and fell to her knees beside him. "Gerry, can ya hear me, son?" He looked at her.

"Yeah."

His father said to his other sons, "Let's get him in the car," and turned to Charlie May. "Thank you, ma'am, fer everthing you done. Them boys told me what you done, too, Perk, and I'm much obliged. Come on now, and we'll take ya home."

Charlie May watched them load into the car and pull away. The tail lights cast a red glow on the muddy yard and she saw something in the driveway, an envelope or something. *Howard must have dropped something. Oh well, I'll get it tomorrow,* she thought as she closed the heavy wooden door.

Charlie May Simon

261

Simon cabin, circa 1931

The outlaw Andrew Miller (right) and his wife (left.)

Hollis Country Store

South Fourche LaFave Bridge at Hollis

265

Hawks School

Forked Mountain

Actual photograph taken by the author from the tree stand.

* Cover photo is the original cabin on the author's property at Hollis.

Bibliography

1 Arkansas Historic Preservation Program
http://www.arkansaspreservation.com/

2"Charlie May Simon," *Encyclopedia of Arkansas History and Culture*
http://www.encyclopediaofarkansas.net/encyclopedia/entry-detail.aspx?search=1&entryID=41 (accessed 1/31/2013.)

3"Civilian Conservation Corps (CCC) *Encyclopedia of Arkansas History and Culture.*
http://www.encyclopediaofarkansas.net/encyclopedia/entry-detail.aspx?entryID=2396 (accessed 2/3/2013.

4 Arkansas Historic Preservation Program
http://www.arkansaspreservation.com/

5"Fourche LaFave River" Encyclopedia of Arkansas History and Culture,
http://www.encyclopediaofarkansas.net/encyclopedia/entry-detail.aspx?entryID=6247 (accessed 2/7/2013)

6http://www.archives.gov/education/lessons/homestead-act

7http://en.wikipedia.org/wiki/Dogtrot_house

8 A tol'able plenty : pioneer farm life in the Ouachita Mountains of Arkansas

by Dunnahoo, Patrick. Publication Date 1982

29343768R00158

Made in the USA
Charleston, SC
10 May 2014